SPIRITUAL DANCE AND WALK

OTHER TITLES BY SAMUEL L. LEWIS

The Rejected Avatar
The Jerusalem Trilogy: Song of the Prophets
Siva! Siva! / Crescent & Heart
Talks of an American Sufi
Introduction to Spiritual Brotherhood:
Science, Mysticism & the New Age
SufiVision and Initiation:
Meetings with Remarkable Beings
The Book of Peace
Original Dances of Universal Peace of Samuel L. Lewis

SPIRITUALDANCE

A N D

WALK

*An Introduction to the
Dances of Universal Peace
and Walking Meditations of*
Samuel L. Lewis

sm

PEACEWORKS
INTERNATIONAL NETWORK FOR THE DANCES OF UNIVERSAL PEACE
SEATTLE, WASHINGTON, USA

First Edition
Second Printing, Revised 1993
Third Printing, Revised 1998

Portions of this work appeared in earlier editions
printed in 1978 and 1983
All writings of Murshid Samuel L. Lewis are copyright 1975/
1990 Sufi Islamia Ruhaniat Society

Dances of Universal Peace in this publication are copyright
1975/1990 International Center for the Dances of Universal Peace.
Permission to reprint or record must be obtained from the
publisher:
PeaceWorks
International Center for the Dances of Universal Peace
444 NE Ravenna Blvd., Suite 3̶0̶6̶ 202
Seattle, WA 98115-6467 USA
Email: peaceworks@compuserve.com
http://www.dancesofuniversalpeace.org

Printed in the United States of America.

Grateful acknowledgement is made to *Creation Spirituality*, the
magazine of the Friends of Creation Spirituality, for permission to
reprint the article "We Circle Around", by Neil Douglas-Klotz

Cover illustration: Violetta Reiser
Cover design: Neil Douglas-Klotz
Text Design: Hassan Herz
Type: Palatino via MacIntosh SE
Text printed on recycled paper

International Standard Book Number 0-915424-13-4
Library of Congress Catalog Card Number 90-60698

Acknowledgements

This edition of *Spiritual Dance and Walk* builds upon the efforts of many people over many years. In addition, we have added a much revised version of the instructions that go with the first volume of music to the Dances. This volume is now called *Dances of Universal Peace I*.

Originally, we planned the Dance instruction section of this book to be released as a separate booklet that would go with our tape. We discovered, however, almost a complete overlap between that material and the Dances included in *Spiritual Dance and Walk*, so the two projects merged. The Dance instructions are substantially edited from those in the comprehensive Teachers Dance Manual. In this case, I found that the descriptions and definitions had to be significantly expanded upon, since in many cases the Teachers Manual reads like a cookbook for those who already know how to cook.

In order to make this an introductory book, we have tried to be as meticulous as possible about definitions of foreign terms and clarity of instruction. Zarifah Demcho-Wagor and I edited the Dances from the Teachers Manual; Zarifah did the middle stage copy editing, I did the initial adding and expanding as well as the final editing. In addition, Zarifah shepherded the dance instruction part of the project through its booklet-stage embryo, acquiring new copies of the music and checking copy with various contributors. Without her, the project could not have been completed.

The revised Dance I tape (and this book) contain six of the earlier Dances which have proven to be mainstays of Dance meetings and which have not been previously recorded: "Benediction Dance", "Kwan Zeon Bosai", "Sat Nam Dance", "Shalom Aleichem"

Murshid Samuel Lewis' original "Nembutsu Dance" and "Ya Hayy Ya Haqq Dance."

This edition also contains an expanded introduction to the writings on Dance and Walk of Murshid Samuel L. Lewis, including the "Ten Lessons on Spiritual Walk", which have been reedited and annotated for clarity.

For typographical and design help as well as much common-sense wisdom over the several editions of *Spiritual Dance and Walk,* many thanks go to Hassan Herz, founder of Prophecy Pressworks and now the director of TBH Typecast in Cotati, California.

The revision and publication of this book were made possible through the truly generous efforts of many individuals; the original members of the Sufi Choir, those who helped to compile, transcribe, and bring into print this material, and all those who gave lovingly of their financial support. Grateful acknowledgement is made to the following for their help in preparing this publication: Moineddin Jablonski, Allaudin Mathieu, Maggie Joy Graham, Violetta Reiser, Danya Veltfort, Wali Ali Meyer, Carol Ardvisura Griffin, Kamae A Miller, Malika Merrill and Zamyat Kirby. Most especially our deepfelt gratitude goes to Murshid Samuel L. Lewis for bringing the Dances of Universal Peace into the world.

—Neil Douglas-Klotz

Contents

I. Writings on Dance and Walk

Editor's Introduction

Seventeen years have passed since the Dances were first introduced to the public in written form in a little booklet entitled *Introduction to Spiritual Dance and Walk*. Fourteen years have passed since the first instruction booklet was published to accompany the *Sufi Dance and Song Album* (revised in 1988 and renamed *Dances of Universal Peace, Volume I*). These years have seen a continued interest and growth in the Dances of Universal Peace. Reaching far beyond the boundaries of the Sufi community, these Dances have given birth to many Dance meetings across the world. In 1988, the Dances were first introduced into the U.S.S.R. during a citizen diplomacy trip that brought Soviets and Americans together to dance for and in peace.

In 1986 this publisher released large portions of Samuel L. Lewis' unpublished diaries in the book *Sufi Vision and Initiation*. This book made clear that Lewis' original vision of the "Dance of Universal Peace" communicated not only the universality of mystical experience behind all religious traditions, but also the importance of bringing to the world "peace through the arts."

Samuel Lewis studied Sufism under Pir-O-Murshid Hazrat Inayat Khan as well as various Sufis in Egypt, Bangladesh, Pakistan and India. He was recognized several times over as a "Sufi"— formally, one who has accomplished the path of being free from distinctions and differences—and as a teacher of Sufism. The depth of his realization of this school can be seen in his more formal commentaries on Sufi mysticism, which are scheduled for release in the coming years. A small portion of one of these commentaries—a section on "The Coming Universality"—is included at the end of the first part of this book.

It should also be remembered that Lewis studied extensively and was recognized as a "Zen-shi," or teacher of Zen Buddhism. He also studied and was recognized as a teacher of Bhakti yoga (under Swami Papa Ramdas), of Christian mysticism (as one of the founders of the Holy Order of M.A.N.S.) and of Hebrew Kaballah. By his own words, it was not his desire to associate his peace work or his Dances with any particular sect:

"Divine truth does not belong to any organization. If I organize here, it will be under the title of "Islamia Ruhaniat Society," that is, the complete teachings of spiritual sciences which lead to realization of peace. As I'm working with my colleagues in other faiths, this will demonstrate this. We're not going to be called "Sufis" to distinguish ourselves from somebody else." (April 18, 1968)

"I do not believe you have to become a Sufi devotee to become perfect. I find perfection in the devotees of many paths.... My friends include many realized souls of many faiths, and I can substantiate this with facts, not emotions." (November 9, 1969)

In addition, Samuel Lewis dedicated the first Dance of Universal Peace to his sacred dance teacher, Ruth St. Denis, and gives her equal credit with Hazrat Inayat Khan for their inspiration. Ruth St. Denis, one of the pioneers of modern American dance (being a teacher of Martha Graham and Doris Humphrey) devoted most of her life to investigating forms of sacred dance that would transform both worship and the arts. It was from her that Samuel Lewis caught the importance of re-visioning a form of American sacred dance which could be shared in groups:

"Ruth St. Denis has the faculty of drawing music and dances right out of the cosmos, out of the heart-of-God. She has taught me this faculty. Not many people can do this, but with the 'coming race' appearing, more and more are coming into incarnation...."

"On my next trip south I am to see, God willing, Ruth St. Denis to present to her the "Dance of Universal Peace." This has been accepted by *world leaders of religion and been rejected by cult leaders. As Miss Ruth and I commune, it is not necessary to say much. She wanted to tell me her philosophy, and I said, 'All right, you speak and I'll dance.' That made her very happy."* (February 27, 1966)

"My fairy godmother, so to speak, Ruth St. Denis, approved of all my plans, and before she left the world I had begun my 'Dances of Universal Peace.' I started out with Dervish Dances, then Indian ones. Now I am ready to restore or start Christian mystical dances. These dances are dedicated to the Temple of Understanding in Washington D.C., which is endeavoring to take to heart the psalmist's words, 'My house shall be a house of prayer for all peoples.'" (July 28, 1970)

It is doubtful that Samuel Lewis would have approved of overlooking these roots of the Dances in favor of the expedient use of the term "Sufi Dancing," which shortly after his passing came to mean any form of semi-organized circle dancing with a "new-age" flavor. Samuel Lewis was very serious about the transformative power of joy and devotion in a universal context, and he was very joyful about presenting the necessary discipline and embodiment needed to make the Dances of Universal Peace more than a "temporary high." While Samuel Lewis was committed to a program of "joy without drugs" with his early hippie disciples, he did not intend that spiritual practice—dance, walk, meditation or chanting—be used as another form of drug or avoidance of real growth. "By their fruits ye shall know them" seems to be the only touchstone for use in this area.

This newly expanded edition of *Spiritual Dance and Walk* gathers a number of previously unpublished writings on spiritual dance and the walking practices that Samuel Lewis began. As the Dances have evolved further, the need has increased for these writings to be available to those around the world who wish to "join the dance." Murshid's writings emphasize the need to embody the states of expanded consciousness which the Dances produce through actual service to the world and work on one's inner growth.

In this regard, Samuel Lewis' vision of peace—both inside and out—demands a passion for growth and change that does not stop

[13]

with the self-satisfaction of "being high." As wonderful as the Dances are, Lewis also emphasized the practices of spiritual walking meditation which allow one to probe the depths of her or his being and discover how to fully embody and live from the place of peace that the Dances allow us to taste.

"My peace theme: eat, dance and pray together."

Like the Dances themselves, Murshid Samuel Lewis's writings range from the simple expressions of practical wisdom to the most subtle, thought-provoking themes suitable for a lifetime of work. This new volume indicates just how broad the heart-capacity of Murshid's vision was. Included here are both selections from his diaries as the initial Dances were coming through—exuberant words of a creation being birthed—to a selection from the long, concentrated work on Spiritual Dancing written in the 1940's that prepared the field and planted the seeds of creation. We hope in the future to bring the whole latter manuscript to print, with appropriate notes and commentaries.

The first part of the book begins with two articles on the Dance—one an overview of their history, another a remembrance of the early days of Dance with Murshid. As noted, the second part of the book serves as a practical introduction to the early Dances and provides the movements and music for all of the Dances on the first anthology recording *Dances of Universal Peace I,* first released in 1975. Six additional early Dances have been added to this recording and these are also reflected in the book.

As you will note, the majority of the early Dances use either sacred phrases in Arabic or Sanskrit. As described in Moineddin Jablonski's article, the first Dances that Samuel Lewis brought through were what he called "Dervish" or "Mantric." He then moved into the area of Christian, "Angelic" and "Mystery" dances with the vision that the range of traditions expressed would expand. He did not finish very many of these latter dances, and the success of his transmission has been that this work has been continued by those who followed. There are probably now in the neighborhood of 350 Dances of Universal Peace created using

[14]

Murshid's original method—concentration and focus on the sacred phrase. The chapter on "Movement and Stillness" contains invaluable keys to this process; in addition, attunement to the living presence of the Dances, deep inner devotion and help from those who are more experienced enables students to learn how to "draw Dances out of the cosmos."

For this reason, the Dances continue to grow in breadth as well as depth. They will perhaps always be a "work in progress" and are relatively young when compared with other traditional sacred dance forms, for instance, the 600-year-old Mevlevi Sema (the formal "whirling" of the Turkish Sufis). The latter practice has become very fomalized over the course of time. This person sees the Dances of Universal Peace continuing to evolve in several directions in the future:

1. They will continue to be used in the training of Sufi disciples on a formal esoteric path of initiation. As such the Dances represent a deep course of development in the sciences of breath, heart, sound, meditation and concentration—all embodied through movement.

2. The Dances have also been given to the world to be "danced free forever." They now play a large part in many gatherings devoted to peace on earth, as more and more people unite in this concern. The Dances are also being recognized for their transformative power by many therapists and educators and are being integrated into settings where the need for self-discovery and unlearning old habits are valued. In these settings, the Dances range far beyond sectarian forms, which in many ways is the fulfillment of Murshid's vision.

The International Network for the Dances of Universal Peace was organized in 1982 to further the work begun by Samuel Lewis with the Dances of Universal Peace and to help make the Dances available to all people. It is the coordinating hub that links the many worldwide Dance circles. The Network:

• provides a registry of all Dance meetings and Dance leaders for networking and referrals;

•publishes a newsletter for members that shares Dance news from around the world;

•sponsors Dance workshops and events for those seeking extended Dance experiences and leadership training;

•maintains archives of the Dances of Universal Peace and notates and records Dance movements, words and music;

•publishes, distributes and sells Dance booklets and tapes and other instructional works related to the Dances;

•cultivates a cooperatively-structured organization through which individuals may grow in openness, honesty, insight, love, flexibility, creativity, accountability and compassion as we work for the benefit of the world family.

May all beings be well! May all beings be happy! Peace! Peace! Peace!

—Neil Douglas-Klotz (Saadi), March 1989

CHAPTER ONE

A Short History of the Dances

We Circle Around, We Circle Around

The story of a Western "peace movement," stemming from the turn of the century, that aims to spread global peace and security from the inside out.

By Neil Douglas-Klotz

"We circle around, We circle around,
the boundaries of the earth, the boundaries of the earth...."
The words of the Arapaho Ghost Dance echo through a hall crowded with people who sing, hold hands and move in concentric circles. Like the original Ghost Dancers, these dancers focus their movement and voices on bringing peace and justice to earth. The folk dance that they do is a collaborative creation of Native American elders and whites. It is one of 300 or so Dances of Universal Peace which invoke all the major traditions of humankind — a non-elitist form of sacred dance that aims to bring "peace-movement" to the planet.

Over the last two years (1988-89) the Dances travelled to and took root in the U.S.S.R., bringing Soviets and Americans together, singing and dancing in celebration of cultural diversity and world peace. Since their founding 22 years ago in San Francisco, the Dances of Universal Peace have been shared in groups throughout the English-speaking world, Costa Rica, Mexico, Holland, Switzerland, Germany, France, Yugoslavia, Turkey, Pakistan and India. As they spread, they bring an experience of praying and dancing in celebration of diversity and in honor of the unity of all creatures.

As a form of "art for peace," the Dances have their origin much earlier in the work of three mystics—two Americans and an Indian—who looked behind the "wars and rumors of war" that they saw in the 1920's to find a deeper basis for peace and global security. From their early work, the Dances of Universal peace have developed, not only as a visible "peace demonstration," but also as a form of therapeutic movement re-education—a way to heal the personal as well as global roots of war and peace.

The Goose-step and War

"Metaphysically, the goose-step and war are one. It makes use of force without stint or qualification. It involves destructive psychic as well as physical forces. To abolish war we must abolish war-like movements."

In 1939, the founder of the Dances of Universal Peace, Samuel L. Lewis, wrote these words as he contemplated the inner realities of sacred dance and its uses in the service of world peace. He was ahead of his time in such thoughts. Lewis, born in 1896 in San Francisco, had early been rejected by his family for an over-avid interest in religion (his father wanted to install him in business) and had studied theosophy, Eastern religions, and the mystical side of his own religion, Judaism. To this end, he sought out and found a wide range of genuine teachers of Buddhism, Vedanta, Yoga and Sufism who made their way to this country during the 'teens and early twenties. During this time, he also studied sacred dance with American dance pioneer Ruth St. Denis (also the teacher of Martha Graham, Doris Humphrey and others).

After reconciling with his father on his deathbed, Lewis received a small inheritance while in his 50's. He finished college with a degree in horticulture and set off on two trips to the East to share the latest in organic farming techniques as well as in search of genuine mysticism. The story of these trips to Japan, India, Pakistan, and Egypt is told in the book of his selected diaries, Sufi Vision and Initiation.

The journeys were pivotal in Lewis's life. Rejected as an "eccentric" at home, on his one-man citizen diplomacy mission, Lewis received welcomes everywhere—from heads of state to the street children for whom he danced. He found that the professors of agricultural colleges were under intense pressure to convert to "modern Western" methods, which were fatally tied in to petroleum-based economies and sterile seed sources. They were enthusiastic about the information and seeds that Lewis pulled from his suitcase. On his search for genuine mystics, Lewis found scientists, scholars, government and professional people at all levels who were practitioners of Zen, Sufism, Vedanta, mystical Christianity and other traditions, but who had been overlooked by Western scholars because they were living what appeared to be "normal lives."

A "Dance of Universal Peace"

Lewis felt confirmed in his early intuition that real religion must be practical and express the deep unity that is found behind all traditions. While at the tomb of a Sufi saint in India, he had a vision of a "Dance of Universal Peace," which would combine mystical practice with a body-based reality of world peace. In his later diaries, Lewis spoke of his understanding of the oft-used word peace:

"Words are not peace. Thoughts are not peace. Plans are not peace. Programs are not peace. Peace is fundamental. It is easy to prove in the sciences, and the real spiritual masters who are here are teaching it. It is fundamental to all faiths, all religions, all spirituality. It is from this that everything was, or let us say: In the beginning was Peace and the Peace was with God and the Peace was God, and out of this Peace has everything been made that was made.

"The difference between this Logos-Peace and what we generally call "peace" is that the latter is a vacuum, a zero, a nothing, a blank, a negative to the extreme. The Logos-Peace is fullness, all-inclusive, and expresses the human family. The human body is a society of myriads of cell units working together. The totality of humanity (adam in Hebrew) is a society of myriads of personalities which must work together in and with and under God. Only this must be experiences and not syllogism, truth and not truism. Every transcendentalist poet of America knew it, every newsman seems to work against it—we must have excitement. Excitement is the death of peace. I have my poetry, and the Dance of Universal Peace."

The Grandmother of the Dance

Upon his return from the East, Lewis dedicated the first Dance of Universal Peace to his sacred dance teacher, Ruth St. Denis, then in her late eighties. A sensation in her early years with individual dances like Radha and Incense, Ruth St. Denis entered the inner realization of the figures of divinity that she chose to perform—like Mary, Kwan Yin, the Yogi, O-Mika and others—and from that feeling danced a vision of perfection. By choosing figures from many different cultures, Ruth St. Denis presented a wordless show of unity before thousands of audiences all over the world throughout her life.

With her partner Ted Shawn, she also founded one of the first schools of modern dance in America, called "Denishawn." Because most of her writings on dance were mystical in nature, she has met with little understanding or favor among contemporary dance historians, who largely overlook her role in creating (along with Isadora Duncan) the first Western modern dance.

When her style of dance fell out of popular favor, Ruth St. Denis retreated to the further investigation of her first love—sacred dance. Among other things, she wished to find a group form of dance that would be easily accessible to non-performers and which would communicate the deep feelings of unity and peace that she had felt in individual performances. It was here that she found a collaborator and apt student in Samuel Lewis. In her unpublished book The Divine Dance (1933), Ruth St. Denis wrote of her vision of a future dance—for life and peace:

"The dance of the future will no longer be concerned with meaningless dexterities of the body.... Remembering that man is indeed the microcosm, the universe in miniature, the Divine Dance of the future should be able to convey with its slightest gestures some significance of the universe.... As we rise higher in the understanding of ourselves, the national and racial dissonances will be forgotten in the universal rhythms of Truth and Love. We shall sense our unity with all peoples who are moving to that exalted rhythm."

The Unity of Religious Ideals

Ruth St. Denis was overjoyed with the promise of a universal sacred folk dance that Lewis presented to her. A few years later, Samuel Lewis, then in his seventies, found a group of people who were willing to embody his vision of dance: the young people and hippies of the late sixties in San Francisco. Along with his Dances, he presented a universal approach to the teachings of Buddhism, Hinduism, Sufism, Christianity and all religions and became known as "Sufi Sam."

Lewis states in his diaries that the other major influence on the Dances of Universal Peace was his first Sufi teacher, Hazrat Inayat Khan (1882 -1927). Hazrat Inayat Khan presented a vision of the "Unity of Religious Ideals" that became a foundation for the Dances and the means of including an ever-widening world of traditions that are celebrated. For Hazrat Inayat Khan, it was important that the issue of religious strife be acknowledged, not swept under the rug with a sort of bland agnosticism or a philosophy that ignores the importance of the religious idealism in life. He wrote:

"Whenever there has been a war...we always see the finger of religion. People think that the reason for war is mostly political, but religion is a greater warmonger than any political ideas. Those who give their lives for an ideal always show some touch of religion. The religious channel in Sufism exists in order to avoid greater catastrophes, and to gather together the followers of different religions in the understanding of the one truth behind them, so that they may hold in respect all the teachers of humanity who have given their lives in the service of truth. Instead of doing as the theologians in colleges who only want to find what is the difference between Moses and Buddha, one should look behind all religions to see where they unite, to find out how the followers of all the different religions can be friends."

In addition, Lewis had learned from Hazrat Inayat Khan the Sufi science of the mysticism of sound, which enabled him to choose phrases for the early Dances which filled the body with resonance and with a genuine feeling for each tradition celebrated. For this reason, he credited both Ruth St. Denis and Hazrat Inayat Khan with providing him the "keys" to the creation of the Dances. Lewis's collaboration with Hazrat Inayat Khan's son, Pir Vilayat Inayat Khan, also proved instrumental in bringing the Dances out of their visionary state and into actuality.

Still a Dance of the Future

After Lewis's passing in 1971, the Dances continued and, because they were often passed by word of mouth, sometimes became confused—in both feeling and form. At one point, any vaguely circular form of group dance with chanting became known as "Sufi dancing," whether those leading them were Sufis or not (and whether they were moving in rhythm or not—the definition of "dancing"). On the positive side, there was an emphasis on simple movement with feeling and thought united. On the negative side, the form was (and still is) sometimes imitated without the necessary training, background or awareness.

Seven years ago, an international Dance network was established to alleviate some of these difficulties and provide access to skills and teaching materials for those who wish to share the Dances in their communities. As more and more people have studied and attuned to the form, new Dances continue to be created and their uses have widened—from peace studies classes to work with the mentally handicapped. The Dances continue to grow for several reasons:

1. The feeling of chanting simple, sacred phrases with devotion—in English, Greek, Latin, Aramaic, Hebrew, Arabic, Sanskrit and many other languages—gives, especially when combined with movement, an immediate, accessible feeling for another tradition. That same feeling may also, as Lewis stated, unearth the forgotten and rejected places within our own cells and psyches.

2. The Dances use simple folk movements drawn from the world's traditions and generated from the feelings of the phrases. The folk movements create a feeling of solidarity and unity. In addition, free movements are used within some dances to allow one to "re-create" one's own authentic movement within the support of the group movement. As contrasted with traditional dance therapy, this is a more effective way to allow participants to experience new creativity and freedom in the body than the elusive exploration of habitual movement and personal neuroticism.

3. The Dances are non-elitist, take no special training and can be done by almost anyone—they have even been done by those in wheelchairs. The miracle of group feeling and joy of the dance is available to "non-dancers." At the same time, the form lends itself to increasing refinement of movement, feeling and body awareness as one simultaneously discovers more of oneself—and more of the world. Combined with forms of walking meditation and exploration that Lewis began, the Dances lead to a confrontation with and acceptance of more and more of one's true self. This is "peace and security" on a body level.

Samuel Lewis envisioned that forms like the Dances of Universal Peace would become the future of the arts—emphasizing group unity rather than the adulation of individuals, process rather than product. He wrote in 1939:

"The Dance is the way of life; the Dance is the sway of life. What life gives may be expressed with body, heart and soul to the glory of God and the elevation of humanity, leading therein to ecstasy and self-realization. VERILY, THIS IS THE SACRED DANCE.

"When doctrines divide and 'isms' turn human against human, without speech, without silence, let us demonstrate. Let these demonstrations manifest everywhere. Not what we think or say but what we do shall avail.... On with the dance!"

[*The preceding article first appeared in* Creation *magazine in the Spring of 1988.*]

CHAPTER TWO

The Early Days of the Dances

by Moineddin Jablonski

It is the late sixties and within the castle-like walls of Scott Hall (a big round tower of the Presbyterian Seminary which overlooks San Anselmo in Marin County) a voice rings out loud and clear:

"Everyone form a circle!"

Not everyone has arrived yet, but a few of the youthful ex-hippies begin to link hands. Others present for the first time are still standing around.

"I said everyone form a circle!"

After the second ringing command, the circle is rapidly formed. The leader of the meeting is Murshid Samuel L. Lewis, a spiritual teacher in the Sufi tradition, who is introducing his audience of young seekers to the Dances of Universal Peace. In a few moments, Murshid formally opens the meeting, asking everyone to recite the Sufi Invocation:

"Toward the One, the Perfection of Love, Harmony and Beauty, the Only Being, United with all the Illuminated Souls who form the Embodiment of the Master, the Spirit of Guidance."

There is a short silence.

"Now let's repeat the Bismillah.... Bismillah, er-Rahman, er-Rahim. We begin in the Name of Allah, Most Merciful and

Compassionate."

The Dancing begins. Throughout the evening the Names of God penetrate and fill the space, building an atmosphere of joy. The Dance arena becomes peaceful, bringing everyone out of the 'realism' of surface life and into the reality of heart, through chanting God's Names.

The Dances of Universal Peace, a compendium of group-dances set to sacred phrases from the various world religions, came to and through Murshid during the last seven years of his life. These Dances have continued to come in inspiration through his followers since his passing on January 15, 1971.

Starting in the spring of 1969, Murshid began getting less and less sleep at night due to the increasing activity of his visionary consciousness. As Murshid put it: "Allah (God) keeps me up at night so I can receive these visions of new Dances." Often it would take two or three days before a Dance which Murshid had witnessed in vision would filter down to the mental realm, to be later translated into written instruction.

The first few Dances that came were simple follow-the-leader type Dances using either "Allah, Allah" or "Om Sri Ram Jai Ram Jai Jai Ram" as the kindling phrase, the Divine Name of God which stands at the center of the Dances. In Murshid's own words he gives the secret:

"No dance is a Spiritual Dance because it is called that; it does not mean a certain form or technique, nor a ritual. What must remain is the sacred phrase; this, the sacred phrase, and not the form, is the foundation of development along this line."

Gradually other movements were added, mostly drawn from different folk-dances Murshid knew, for he had been a diligent folk-dance aficionado earlier in his life. Murshid said he was actually very timid as a youth and that he joined a folk-dance club to overcome his shyness. He used folk-dance movements from all over the world, borrowing from places he had visited during his trips abroad in 1956 and again in 1962.

As was Murshid's manner, he wrote incessantly to his old friends to let them know the astounding new developments in his life, friends who like Murshid were in their sixties and seventies. Many of his old friends congratulated him, some merely wrote his remarks off as the antics of an already eccentric man, while the young people began to experience more and more the well of baraka (Arabic for the magnetic love-blessings which impregnate a mystic's atmosphere) that had long remained untapped through a lifelong pattern of rejection by his peers.

At the same time, Murshid cultivated a steady correspondence with humor columnist Art Hoppe of the San Francisco *Chronicle* and wrote repeatedly with tongue-in-cheek: "Art, I have failed miserably as a Pied Piper. Only the young show up!"

Finally, Murshid's old folk-dance club invited him to bring his group of young ex-hippies (Murshid's term) to perform for the club's special anniversary celebration. This was the first public performance of the Dances of Universal Peace. Later, public performances of the Dances were to occur in Precita Park opposite the Mentorgarten, Murshid's San Francisco home, and in cathedrals and temples in California and elsewhere since his passing. In fact, the Dances are now an international phenomenon.

By the time Murshid visited Los Angeles in June of 1969 with two of his disciples, several new Dances had become regular features at the weekly meetings. He wasted no time demonstrating (or 'angel-strating' as he would pun) these new Dances with just three people, himself and his two students, for his Los Angeles friends—right in their living rooms! Murshid wasn't the type to let such behavior fall short of its intended purpose, even if it proved momentarily embarrassing to his hosts. If they were still Murshid's friends this late in life, they were probably used to it. His young followers took everything mostly in stride, although a few doses of social embarrassment at the hands of Murshid were always in store!

The legendary Ruth St. Denis, whom Murshid referred to as his 'fairy godmother,' played the role of confirming angel in his efforts to gain support for the Dances. It was after Murshid visited the tomb of Sheikh Selim Chisti, a Sufi Saint, at Fathepur Sikri in India that he began his Dance work in earnest. Murshid had entered a state of mystical absorption wherein the theme "Dance of Universal Peace" was disclosed. At the tombsite he performed his first attempt of the Dance of Universal Peace in which man, incorporating the religious expressions of his race through millennia, dances in devotion to God and God dances with loving compassion through man.

When Murshid returned to this country he visited "Miss Ruth" and said,

"Srimati (Mother Divine), I have the answer to all the world's problems."

"What is it?" she asked.

"I'm going to teach little children how to Walk," he replied.

"You've got it, you've got it, you've got it!" exclaimed Miss Ruth.

Murshid felt that basic rhythms should be introduced to children early in life, and that training in Walk could be part of every child's upbringing, without any somber overtones. With this happily applied training in Walk, it would be a matter of but another step and the Dance could unfold with full consciousness.

He would remark to Miss Ruth: "You taught me how to draw these Dances right out of the cosmos, right from the space." Miss Ruth had inspired Murshid not only to continue his efforts to spread Spiritual Dancing, but also to attune to the dance-ful moods and modes in the atmosphere within and around us, and to bring the inspirations into manifest portrayal.

Back in January of 1967, shortly after the first few ex(ing)-hippies discovered Murshid living in a two-room apartment on Clementina Street, an alleyway south of Market Street, Murshid suffered what he termed "an attack of food-poisoning." Later, another friend told us that Murshid had actually had a heart-attack, but he didn't want his young disciples to know it was that serious. At the time of his attack there were about ten disciples who attended his talks regularly. When he took sick we prepared to visit him at the Chinese Hospital (the same hospital where he was later to die) on Jackson Street. When we got there Murshid was ashen-faced and could hardly talk. Murshid's lifelong friend Joe Miller was there with his wife Guin. Joe tried to pep Murshid up with a few well-chosen words. Dr. Ajari Warwick, a Zen teacher, was there from time to time, and Murshid later said it may have been Dr. Warwick's healing puja ceremony—performed on the spot—that helped spur him back to physical health.

It was that hospital stay that Murshid would speak of later:

"There I was flat on my back in the hospital and Allah decides that is when He is going to manifest, when I have no choice but to accept!"

Then Murshid went on to describe the vision vouchsafed to him:

"I saw a mountain at the top of which there was a little trickle of water, and, after the water had gone down the slope a little bit, it became a sizeable stream. Then the stream became a rushing river, which in turn became a mighty river with several tributaries. As the river neared the plain the flowing water was so strong it could not be stopped, and would continue to flow until it merged into the ocean."

"Do you know what that means?" Murshid would ask. Then he would answer:

"It means that I have completed my first stage as a spiritual teacher—that's the little trickle at the top. Next will be the period of expanding to thirty disciples. And after that to sixty and after that to a hundred disciples. Then, after the vision, God says to me, 'I make you spiritual leader of the hippies.'"

Through the trial of near-death Murshid emerged stronger than before, and declared that the promise of spiritual unfoldment for him together with his disciples was a confirmation of the commission he had received five years earlier from his Pir-O-Murshid (Sufi teacher) in Pakistan: "You will cause fifty thousand Americans to chant 'Allah'." We little realized how joyous a way Murshid would provide for us and the world when he gave out the Dances.

It has been four years since Murshid's passing, years which have witnessed an increase in the repertoire of the Dances, the quality now developing beyond the rough-hewn manner we were capable of in the beginning, and the scope of the Dances now opening to a world perspective. Murshid saw this development shortly before he left the world and expressed his vision to the Women's Dance Class, a group of women disciples who met for the purpose of refining the Dances, inaugurating more graceful movements to coordinate the similarly refined singing of God's Names:

"The next step will be to establish Jewish and Christian Dances. We already have Mantric Dances, Dervish Dances and Mystery Dances. After that we will have Dances for all religions. And then we will begin to work on having Angelic Dances, Dances which will take you very high."

These Dances have come, are coming, and with them an ability to deepen the Dance experience with both new and old Dances. It would not be proper to say that the Angelic Dances are too different from other types of sacred Dances. Angelic Dances simply express the exaltation in all of us which comes when our human limitations are overcome through an act of blessing another, or through losing oneself in the love (which asks for no return) of another. So really every Dance can be an Angelic Dance, yet there are certain sacred phrases, certain movements of grace, which promote the utterly translucent Angelic moods hidden within us.

But there may be even deeper experiences open to the Spiritual Dancer. Murshid has written in Suras of the New Age; "When the Dervish whirls, the Angels tremble." This shows that the Angels can become entrapped by a devotion which sees God as if through a window-glass, while the Dervish, or Sufi has, like Shiva or Krishna, become identical with God through dancing The Dance which illuminates and integrates all planes of our being, all aspects of our personality from the seen to the Unseen.

"THE WATCHER IS THE PRAYERFUL DEVOTEE,
BUT THE DANCER BECOMES DIVINE."
(from Murshid's poem *Siva, Siva*)

To dance the Divine Dance we can follow the footsteps of the Masters, Saints and Prophets of humanity. We can dance the Dance of the Divine Messengers, giving to all the blessing of God which we see naturally in a loving mother, a kind father, an innocent child, a helpful friend and in an inspiring teacher. We can dance to improve ourselves; we can dance to overcome ourselves. We can even dance to find ourselves.

All these purposes of Spiritual Dancing are answered when we begin to feel the Divine Presence more and more as we dance.

This is being offered in the hope that multitudes of people will be able to take up the Dances of Universal Peace in a real way, by remaining centered and confident in the endeavor toward fuller awakening.

[*The preceding first appeared as the introduction to the booklet accompanying the* Sufi Dance and Song Album *published in 1975.]*

CHAPTER THREE

Letters to Anandashram

"The Dances are Rushing to Sam..."

[During his life, Samuel L. Lewis studied with many spiritual teachers of various traditions. His major heart-connection to mystical Hinduism was Swami Papa Ramdas. Ramdas, through his many travels and lectures, popularized the sacred mantra Om Sri Ram Jai Ram Jai Jai Ram. *When Swami Ramdas passed in 1965, his student Mother Krishnabai continued his work at Anandashram near Kanhangad in South India. Samuel Lewis once called her "the most spiritual being" he had ever met. Mother Krishnabai passed from this world in February 1989.*

In honor of her passing, we note the important role that both she and Papa Ramdas played in the inspiration of the Dances of Universal Peace and include here excerpts from the letters that Murshid Samuel Lewis wrote to Anandashram during the creative rush of Dances he experienced from 1968-70. In keeping with Swami Ramdas' own style of correspondence, Murshid refers to himself in the third person as "Sam" (indicating that on one level he is an impersonal channel for the Dances), which was also an acronym for his Sufi spiritual name: Sufi Ahmed Murad— S.A.M.-ed.]

June 12, 1968: "We use the Divine Name, we use the Zikar and Ram Nam, all the time. They work. They take us from mortality to immortality."

November 7, 1968: "The repetitions of the names of God, mostly Arabic and Sanskrit, are the basis of all the new dances coming through Sam. In fact, you cannot do them without repeating the divine names. The result on the emotions is revolutionary."

December 18, 1968: "There are signs that through the Dance Sam may become an instrument of Ram in bringing the young to repeat mantras in joy — exactly what is happening more and more."

November 24, 1969: "The difference between us and others is that we use sacred phrases from various religions; that we use arm and other movements of psychic and metaphysical import as if from various religions... So there is before us tremendous areas of dancing, with all kinds of movements, symbols and meanings that we hope to give the world as Ram wills. In a previous report Sam told about the resonance which takes place in singing Ram Nam using the head as a dome. Now the resonance has become more complete, using and vibrating the whole body, demonstrating what is taught, is taught but not studied, in the Christian Bible, 'The human body is the temple of the Holy Spirit.'"

January 4, 1970: "Our work in mantra yoga, our work in cosmic dancing, is being built up and we are succeeding with our song and dance where the verbalists, the intellectuals, the mere exhorters fail. In this sense our praise is towards God or Ram."

January 18, 1970: "We are having more and more Dervish dances, Mantric dances, Yoga dances and increase in joy with balance — not blind ecstasy, but the joy which opens and expands the inner consciousness."

August 14, 1970: "Initiated into the akasha by Hazrat Inayat Khan and Ruth St. Denis who first brought these teachings jointly in 1910, the dances are rushing to Sam all the time."

August 14, 1970: "And God, so to speak, is giving Sam new dances all the time especially Sufi and Ram Nam dances and the young not only love them but are having the effects in greater joy, even ecstasy, and psychic and moral education. But Sam also emphasizes that all great prophets taught almost the same thing and the emphasis on the three-body constitution of man and the utilization first of Love and then Joy and Peace as cosmic attributes and functions are succeeding."

September 15, 1970: "Every night is like a continuous stage performance of spiritual dances. Nearly all of them are based on the Ramnam or Sufi Zikar...Since the Divine diksha [Hindu term, initiation], Sam has had hardly any sleep. He closes his eyes and there is a Divine Dance. So many Divine Dances all the time."

December 6, 1970: "Sam is taking all the elements he knows of Western dancing and amalgamating them with the Names of God and praise of God. It is both devotion and science, because although the motif is toward Holiness, it seems to bring out at the same time Joy, elation, beautiful art forms, and wonderful responses."

CHAPTER FOUR

From Lessons and Diaries

Steps Toward Peace Through Spiritual Dance and Walk

by Murshid Samuel L. Lewis

[The unpublished writings of Dances of Universal Peace founder Samuel L. Lewis present a wealth of direction, inspiration and advice on cultivating the attitude and skills necessary to be a "peace dancer." The following selection draws from his diaries and unpublished lessons for students on the intention behind the Dances, qualities needed for this work and preferences for training in the basic elements of Dance and Walking Meditation. It serves as an introduction to his deeper work on these subjects, a portion of which follows in the next two chapters. Reference letters at the end of each selection refer to papers listed at the end of this article. —ed.]

What Does Dance Do?

What does dance do for us? First and foremost, it inculcates the sense of rhythm and enhances our response to rhythm. This is really a response to life. It makes us more living, which is to say, more spiritual. It brings out beauty of form and movement, and envelopes our personalities in the enjoyment of them. It takes us beyond ourselves, bringing an initial taste of the state of non-being, which is really a balm for the soul. Whether one follows classical, romantic, popular, exotic, Oriental, Occidental or personal models, there is a modicum of intellectual significance added to the dance, so that body, mind and heart can unite.

No doubt we can learn from the Orient and in return can teach Asiatics. If we need anything from India, it is the spirit, particularly that spirit which underlies the sacred dances of that country. We have our peculiar physique, our traditions, our forms. We need abandon nothing. We do not protest against accepted styles. We want to employ everything we can on the pathways toward God-realization. [SD, cir. 1940.]

A Universal Spiritual Revival

We look for a universal spiritual-aesthetic revival. The cultivation of ecstasy and attainment of superconsciousness are steps on the way. We are here to complete our humanity, not to avoid it. Therefore we must hold before ourselves the ideal of the holiness of humanity and the sacredness of the body. Institutions, themes, forms and ideas are inferior to humanity, for humanity was created by God, and these things were made by humanity. As humanity grows in understanding, in consideration and in compassion, spiritual art will unfold itself accordingly. Humanity's heart-awakening must come first.

A warning note should be expressed here. If the dance or any art be cultivated for psychic or magical purposes, the world will not evolve, it will regress. On the other hand, if there is the hoped for spiritual awakening, then all the arts will reach a higher status. Perhaps then the magic, the psychic powers, the unknown forces and faculties will appear as if quite natural. With the coming of the Sovereignty of God in the human heart, many marvels will be added. [SD, cir. 1940].

The Spiritual and the Practical

When we separate the spiritual from the "real," the "practical," the "beautiful," we build a concept which of itself is not spiritual. Our thought of God is not divinity. It is one of the many thoughts of our mind and is less than we. Korzybski has pointed out that the word *p-e-n-c-i-l* is not a writing tool, it is a word. The word *G-o-d* is not the Divine Being, nor is the thought we hold the ultimate reality. Spirituality is beyond word and thought.

The dance revolution proposed goes deeper. It does not abrogate skill, but would offer encouragement to every type of artist. Even burlesque may remain. It does not say of the ballet that its principles are contrary to physiological mechanics. It does not believe that the study and performance of ancient dances should be detached from art and joined to anthropology. All forms and methods would be utilized. Only a sincere feeling for beauty would be demanded.

In and around Hollywood, there is at least one teacher [Ruth St. Denis] whose methods are based upon cardiac mechanics and heart-concentration. Her pupils learn, more or less consciously, to invoke psychic forces. They imbibe philosophy from the dance itself. Their spiritual faculties unfold without anything being said of them. At the same time, they emphasize interpretive rather than program dancing. To them, the right interpretive dance offers full scope to the will of the performer and gives her or him every opportunity for self-expression. [SD, cir. 1940].

Folk Art and Peace

There have been societies in the many places to preserve the folk arts. The harm done to them by this diabolic war [World War II] can never be measured. The folk dances have a direct appeal. Their spirit belongs to the people. They illustrate the dance as an index to human character in accordance with Havelock Ellis' famous question "What do you dance?" [in The Dance of Life, 1929]. When civilization and order are restored, as restored they must be, let us remember that humanity does not live by bread alone. The human spirit needs sustenance. The peacemakers should do their utmost to encourage these arts. [SD, cir. 1940].

Dance and Human Education

We protest against stilted, dynamical geometric patterns which appear so delightful in Hollywood films [in the 20's and 30's]. They turn performers into automata. Even communist Russia has not dehumanized the individual dancer so much as Hollywood has. Those who battle fearlessly against gearing a human to a machine, say to a belt in an automobile factory, should also protest these group-robot dances. Bear in mind the words of Jesus: "Fear not them that torture the body but rather them that torture the soul with hell-fire."

Many stage dances have elements of the group-unit which may become the basis of the new aesthetic and new civilization. Dane Rudhyar has been a sort of modern prophet in this respect. The group-unit may have the fellow-feeling and attunement that might be expected of members of an orchestra. When there is a common spirit in a group, the same psychic currents touch all. There will be a common zest for life. Group silences and concentrations will prove most valuable if we wish to face the new age with sanity.

The art and music appreciation courses in public schools have done something to awaken ideals and ideas in the young. We must not stop there. It is not enough to awaken only the practical or "human" qualities among the young. We must foster genius. Just glance at all the attempted suicides among the young! Ask the psychologists how many more have pondered this fatal step. We must arise beyond the period of crass materialism to a broader outlook. [SD, cir. 1940.]

The Dance, Nervous Energy and Types of Ecstasy

Physical movement alone is sterile and that which does not involve emotion may be excluded from art. The march may be called a dance; it is a rhythmical, physical movement of the body, usually to the accompaniment of music and having a distinct purpose. The march does not demand grace or beauty; in it Yang [the positive element] dominates over Yin [the receptive]. The goose-step is an extreme example.

The Goose-Step involves a maximum of Yang to practically the complete exclusion of Yin. Metaphysically, the Goose-Step and War are one. The Goose-Step is a war march, as much or more than the savage dance is a war dance. It makes use of force without stint or qualification. It involves destructive psychic as well as physical forces. To abolish war we must abolish war-like movements.

Indeed, all bodily movements involve psychic forces which, while operating on the physical plane, are partly magnetic and partly mental. It may be said that they are mental in point of origin and biophysical or bio-electromagnetic in operation. They move along the nervous network and form an aura around it. When the body moves, this aura is extended in the direction of movement, always ahead of the physical center of gravity. It may be said that there is a physical center of gravity in or near the heart, and a psychic center of gravity determined dynamically by the direction of movement. The former is more or less static, the latter dynamic even in repose. For in repose, the psychic field of force may be extended according to the condition of thought and the quality of breath. The understanding of this will help to explain several kinds of metaphysical phenomena, commonly ascribed to spirit communication, etc.

Use and misuse of psychic energy tend toward stimulation or fatigue. When stimulation is under control there is ease and joy. It is a part of life to increase that joy even to the degree of ecstasy. But before the nature of ecstasy can be understood, one must learn the relation of mind to body and of heart to both mind and body. Otherwise, there will be that debilitating false ecstasy which is nothing but psychic inebriation. [SD, cir. 1940.]

Monkey and Cat Methods of Training

Nasik, India—[The "fruit swami"] explained to me the two methods of spiritual training, called the "monkey method" and the "cat method." In the monkey method, the baby holds onto the mother and wherever the mother goes the mother carries the baby. In the cat method, the cat picks up the kitten and teaches it to walk. So the cat tries to make its offspring an adult as soon as it can, and the monkey tries to keep its offspring an infant for as long as it can. So you have two types of spiritual training: those who lean on the teacher to do everything and those who teach their disciples how to become adults. He told me I was on the cat method....[Diaries, 1956].

On the Teaching "Battery"

It is a mistake to asume there is any "teacher." The teacher is the positive pole of a cell and as the pupil or pupils—the negative pole—show more aptitude, the electromagnetic field of the cell increases and knowledge comes through the teacher which would have otherwise been impossible.

In the real samadhi, one has not only union-with-God but with all humanity; when one is helping others, one is helping oneself, and when one is really helping oneself, one is helping others. [Diaries, 1967.]

On Initiating the Spiritual Walks

One has begun teaching spirituality through the Walk. This method was blessed by the late Miss Ruth St. Denis, a very spiritual dancing teacher who knew how to receive inspiration from the very space itself.

The Walk developed in two directions: extentionally and intentionally. In the extentional walk, disciples learned to climb hills and mountains and walk long distances. But then the question arose: if [sacred phrases] could be used to help one walk long distances, climb mountains and work without fatigue, couldn't they be used to help humanity in its greater education, purification and development? So now we use many of the sacred phrases in moral development and psychic purification....

By applying the divine qualities to humanity, one helps to remove the evils, the shortcomings, the impediments and all the grosser aspects of being. A sacred phrase is better than a chastisement.... The next phase seems to be coming—that these methods can be extended to deal with psychological problems. [Diaries, 1970].

Group Training in the Walk

Through the teachings on Walk and many of the Dances, followers of different religions may benefit through stress on their particular ideal. All persons do not have to walk or behave similarly; or as is taught, "unity, not uniformity". In performing the Walks, the grade of development is not necessarily measured by the practice in group. The individual benefits more from his or her own practices, but the community is benefitted by group undertakings.

There is no absolute measurement. Some disciples have had enlightenment experiences through the Walk, either through their own realizations or through the Grace that can manifest. The prayer that we can see God through Grace, Glory, Wisdom, Joy and Peace becomes a reality. [FS, 1970].

Developing Capacity Through Breath and Heart

Every breath raises or lowers the electrical state of the body which can be demonstrated and proven scientifically. If this power is increased without augmenting the capacity many times more—which is done by meditation—the same thing will happen and does happen to the human body as occurs to the electrical system—a fuse blows out and you have trouble....

Capacity is increased by meditation and, in general, by heart action, by maintaining the rhythm of the heartbeat, by feeling the consciousness in the heart, by directing all activity from the center to the circumference and by maintaining unity in feeling, thought and action. It is connected with inspiration. [THSB.]

Divine Mother and Divine Breath

The Mother of the World has two aspects. The first is the accommodation for the planets which is the same as the formation of the ovary with its functions. As the fecundated mother does not menstruate, there is the second aspect of the mother with mammary glands, as Hathor of the Egyptians. Hathor literally means "House of Light." So the Divine Mother after fecundation gave birth to the earth planet and this she nourishes with breath, prana. Therefore Divine Mother and Divine Breath are identified.

So long as one sees from one's limited point of view, one is held in bondage by one's individual breath, thought and emotions. Use of sacred phrases—mantras and wasifas—destroy the hard-making power in the subconscious self or ego, which in enlightened souls becomes identified with the world-self, in other words with the Divine Mother, the Goddess Kali. Looking at life from this point of view, one constructs the Universal Sense in one's spiritual development. Only then can one be called a sage. [THSB.]

[References: SD = "Spiritual Dancing" (unpublished manuscript, written about 1940); Diary entries are included in the autobiographical collection Sufi Vision and Initiation; FS = "Fana-fi-Sheikh" (unpublished paper for initiates); THSB = "Two Hundred and One Suras on Breath" (unpublished paper); TDM = papers published as part of the Teachers Dance Manual.]

CHAPTER FIVE

Ten Lessons on Spiritual Walking Practice

by Murshid Samuel L. Lewis

1. Walk

Walking is one of the first arts which can be taught to children. It is not usually looked upon as an art, but in teaching children how to draw and how to dance, some knowledge of walking as an art or even as a science is helpful. We do not usually take this seriously, and we do not see that without some knowledge, not only uncontrolled fatigue but also emotional problems arise.

The principle of Path appears in several religions, not only in their mystical aspects but in many ceremonies and rituals. Circumambulation of an altar or shrine may even be regarded as an important act of devotion. The very word path signifies that which comes from the feet treading; it almost means "what is footed." It is now important to study the Walk both as a physical exercise and as a super-physical endeavor, making both movement and rest the most fundamental things in life.

No doubt out of Walking came circumambulation and other rituals, and these all culminated in pilgrimages of some sort. In many rituals or pilgrimages the shoes are discarded—sometimes one is even compelled to go barefoot. Moses was told to take off his shoes because he was on holy ground, but both the ritual and the importance of this have been lost in the West.

In Sufism it is stressed that the physical Body is the temple of God. This was also taught by Jesus Christ in both the scriptures and in other writings attributed to him. Why has it been overlooked? Institutions have been made more important than human beings. The non-acceptance of the human being as created in the divine image has set all religion off in the wrong direction.

In the consideration of Walk the feet themselves are connected with shrines. When one does the Lotus and other postures, the human Body is the shrine and the feet are accordingly tucked either under or over the legs. When one uses an external shrine, one may walk around it. But if one agrees with Kabir that God is everywhere, one can learn in Walk that the Body is the real temple and that every place is the holy shrine.

With this attitude we not only learn to Walk but also to overcome fatigue without giving any consideration to the fatigue. The Hebrew Bible states that the Creator does not slumber nor sleep. Not only whoever is conscious of the Divine Presence, but even every organ of the Body, filled with divinity, will be able to function as if belonging to Eternity rather than to time.

2. Breath

It should be recognized that before we can run we must be able to Walk. By the same token, even before we Walk we should be able to breathe; breath is life. As the Western world has developed its own knowledge and sciences without consideration of breath, it is very important to take into account this neglected fundamental of our being.

Breath-currents have energy values as well as chemical and mechanical ones. These are studied in Sufi mysticism and also in the works of Rama Prasad. If one stops breathing, functions also stop, and some Indians identify 'prana,' the breath, with life itself. We cannot say they are wrong; it depends on definition and explanation. But to define does not mean to explain and neither definition nor explanation are the functioning itself.

It cannot be emphasized too much that life depends on breath. Our willing has nothing to do with it. If one ambles, if one slouches, one does not manifest magnetism. From the very beginning of discipleship, talibs [students] in Sufism are given instructions in breathing which aid in increasing both magnetism and the capacity for vitality.

One can understand some of this with music and its effect; especially the effects of marches, whether military or not. They first impel the Body to walk, then to walk in rhythm and thirdly to feel vitality. This gives some idea as to how to increase magnetism. And the first thing which should be learned is to breathe in rhythm.

We can learn from the infants who use rattles and drums and metal objects which supply rhythm. Melody is something else and is concerned with mind. At an early age, before the mind is properly developed, children respond to rhythm and make rhythms themselves.

The use of rhythms help one to walk and to walk properly. The other thing needed is posture. We require posture in repose in the practices of meditation. We require dynamic posture in Spiritual Walk, to have the back straight and the head perpendicular. Someone has written on 'back breathing'; this is proper when the currents go from the base of the spine upward. It has untold advantages and yet is one of the most fundamental and simple things in life.

Therefore one of the first lessons is proper posture, proper breathing, proper rhythm. And these help also to overcome fatigue.

3. Thought

The human Body is such that its operations are associated in some way with the nervous system; in other words, there is no action without involving some kind of thought—conscious, subconscious or even unconscious. Thus also psychic power is involved.

We can learn much from a study of Nature, especially of the animal world. We can learn how the nervous system develops, first into the muscular system, then to the gradual evolution into specialized organs. Anatomy is analytical and does not always help one to understand principles. Physiology is dynamic and sometimes the study of physiology throws light on psychology but the reciprocal is also true. Or as the Buddhists teach, mind and Body are one (not to be accepted too literally).

From Nature we can also understand instinct, although this does not always come through study. Instinct may be called the unconscious or underside of insight. It shows that humanity lives in a universe of mind although it is not necessarily aware of it. This becomes apparent when there is coordination of thought, effort and action; then the personality becomes properly integrated.

It is more necessary to feel than to think about one's movements. Thinking about action alone can become a wearing thought and use up the mental magnetism. But if the mind is permitted to wander too much one can lose direction. Therefore in the practice known as Walking Fikar one must have a particular path, preferably a straight line. It should be in fields or what are called 'jungles' in the Orient, meaning where one does not meet people or vehicles.

If one has a goal, physical or mental, while walking, it brings all the magnetism together. It is a living concentration. For instance a loving person going to meet his or her beloved is endowed and imbued with a living spirit which makes action easier, fatigue disappears. If we practice a "TOWARD THE ONE," whatever be the goal or purpose, walking becomes much easier. Other sacred phrases may also be thought or repeated, consciously or unconsciously.

4. Spiritual Walk

The Spiritual Walk is one connected with esoteric training and development. It may be begun in the Buddhist fashion by simply counting the breaths, a fixed number, or a certain number. Or it may be done in the Sufi fashion which is not too different, except there are accepted cycles like 4, 10, 14, 20, 33, 100 or 101, etc.

Very often it is a good idea to encourage applicants and neophytes to walk and to watch the breath. This is the actual discipline in some Sufi Orders. What is most important is to learn the relationship between God and humanity, between breath and life, and thus pass beyond the gates of so-called death.

Next one should breathe concentrating on "TOWARD THE ONE" with both inhalation and exhalation. This can best be done by "leaning" on the breath—giving it more emphasis— but one can also take so many steps to each breath. This is somewhat more complicated. In between these two stages comes walking while listening to music; in this practice attuning to the rhythm is most important. Those who have had training in meditation and this Darood (TOWARD THE ONE, etc.) will find the latter practice easier and more comfortable. It comes naturally.

As one breathes in and out with the concentration "TOWARD THE ONE," all the essence of the universe can enter with the breath and also all the poisons can go out of the system. If this is not sufficient one can be taught other sacred phrases, but for a group "TOWARD THE ONE" is very good. Besides, a group so joining builds up magnetism. As the group progresses from Spiritual Walk to ceremonial or ritual and from ritual to dance, the dynamics and magnetism of both person and group increase. The capacity also increases for the divine baraka [blessing-magnetism] to manifesting on the earth-sphere.

If this is assigned as a spiritual practice, it should be in blocks of 100 steps, adding one at the end (101, 301, etc.). But in a group, blocks of ten are sufficient— 10, 20, 30, etc.

The group may also benefit from meditation; especially any attendant musician should be skillful in meditation. In the absence of a musician (or musicians), suitable music should be used, not too loud but with definite rhythms which can be easily appreciated.

5. Inhalation and Exhalation

The subject of inhalation and exhalation looks very simple, but it is actually very complicated and important. It sometimes takes years to understand all the activities which benefit when one is inhaling and all the activities which benefit when one is exhaling. This is an important part of mysticism, although athletes will also appreciate it.

In throwing or tossing it is important to work with the exhalation and in receiving or catching with the inhalation. It is also beneficial to learn this from life and not to memorize the series of activities which benefit from inhaling or exhaling. Strange as it may seem, there are also activities which benefit the inhalations and the exhalations. That is to say, there are actions which benefit breaths and there are breaths which benefit actions.

In walking uphill, the inhalation is important. If one loses breath, one loses magnetism; if one controls breath, no magnetism is lost. When one controls breath and magnetism, the probability is that one can walk much longer and take more difficult ascents. However there is nothing to be gained here by trying to show prowess. Regarding the human Body as the divine temple is important. As one gains from the all-pervading power of space every effort at climbing benefits.

There are also schools of esoteric development which utilize mountain climbing. This is more complex than ordinary walking. We cannot compare them for each has its mission and its effectiveness. Symbolically the Path is pictured as going up a mountain and there is much benefit, after people can walk a long time without fatigue, to make an endeavor along this line. There are also pilgrimages to high mountains and any earlier training will prove to be beneficial for those who wish to go to the Andes or other mountains.

As climbing depends mostly on inhalation, so going downhill depends on exhalation. If one exhales properly, one's footing will be more sure. Every step should be an exercise not only of the feet but also of the breath. Pupils should even practice in their rooms so that they are aware of their breath and its connection with all physical movements, but most of all with walking.

If this lesson is given to children when quite young, they will build foundations from which they can benefit all through life. The early formative years are most important. Then the walking practice can develop into games and rituals, and this will make the lessons pleasant.

Both children and adults should be encouraged to stop occasionally, to be assured of their breath. If there is a group or party, the tempo should be as slow as possible to accommodate the slower ones, but not so slow that they become dominant. It is necessary to improve; therefore, attunement with the teacher is most important of all.

Of equal importance is posture. The back should be straight except when climbing requires a partial stoop and descent a partial leaning back. Even here the back should be as straight as possible. One acts as if one were breathing up the backbone. This can be true at all times, and the lessons in meditation must not be lost when the Body is put in motion.

Zen Buddhism says, "Zen is everyday life." It is not so when we make a doctrine of it. It is so when we practice it at all times.

6. Preventing Fatigue

The attributes of God [in Sufi terms, these sacred phrases are called the Sifat -i-Allah] may be used to help overcome any shortcomings. Loss of breath is actually one of the greatest of shortcomings. We do not notice it. We find that many people who are very emotional, who are selfish, who are inconsiderate, do not breath correctly. When we get them to take slow, rhythmical inhalations and exhalations, it has a profound effect on their character. This is because, as the Bible teaches (but unfortunately religion does not accept) "God is Breath."

The phrase "Ya Hayy" [one of the Sifat-i-Allah] may be translated "O Life," but it is not "Life" as a concept or thought. The very vowel efforts show that the life is connected with both breath and vowel formation. People who are subject to fatigue easily, who cannot carry out any project because the mind wanders, benefit by repeating audibly or mentally this phrase, "YA HAYY."

In practice there are two ways to use it. One is on the inhalation: every time one starts to breathe in, one may think this phrase. The other way is to think the phrase every time one takes a step with the right foot. Either method has some advantage.

A slightly more complicated exercise is to think "Ya HAYY YA HAQQ," which roughly means "O Life, O Truth." Actually the "q" or guttural sound helps to bring the effectiveness down to earth. If people often repeat "YA HAYY", they could be drawn above the denseness of earth, even to ecstasy. For many this is good, especially in the material civilization. For the young this is also good, for they live in a less dense atmosphere.

But by repeating in sound or thought "Ya HAYY, YA HAQQ," one keeps balance—not too much inwardness, not too much outwardness. One might almost add that people who are extroverted by nature gain from "YA HAYY" and people who are introverted by "YA HAQQ." For a group it is best to use the phrases together.

In Spiritual Walk, one usually starts by concentrating on the thought of the sacred phrases until one is well aware of their effectiveness— how of themselves they control and magnetize the breath. If this basic lesson is learned, it will help much more when persons or groups advance to rituals and dances.

7. The Use of Centers

Hara is a Japanese word for centering in the navel plexus, the bundle of nerves in the abdominal region. This centering is much used by those who practice meditation. Meditation has been taught sitting in lotus postures, and this often tires or fixates certain muscles. The muscles must be unstrung, this tension should not be allowed to remain too long.

There are lazy people both in the Orient and Occident who

devote much time to sitting. Some even are under the delusion that sitting itself is spiritual emancipation and has a connection with samadhi [the experience of merging with the cosmos]. Nothing could be further from the truth. For the folding in of the Body involves the folding in of the mind.

Sufis use the symbol of the dot and circle for concentration; this is also emblematic of contraction and expansion. The Hara Walk is essentially a contractive Walk, and it brings all the benefits of this contraction. For instance, it helps in concentration, it helps to synthesize and to produce what has been called "integration of personality." Those who practice Hara are certainly of one piece.

They do not have wandering minds. As they keep the Body under control, at the same time they are keeping the mind under control, and this builds up the will. It also makes possible long endeavor and so is another way of overcoming fatigue.

This Hara practice corresponds to the negative or emptying side of the Sufi sacred phrase "LA ILLAHA EL IL ALLAH."[There is no reality, except for Oneness]. This first side [There is no reality...] is called "fana" by Sufis and helps toward self-effacement. It has been assumed, and wrongly assumed, that this negative effacement also produces liberation. That is only one side of it. In any case, no mechanical means, no rules, no rituals, nothing controlled by humanity alone can liberate the human being. Nonetheless, this practice brings the control of nafs, the ego, and its benefits are enormous.

We can read about Hara in books by Japanese (mostly) on Zen. But we can also read (and the superficial writers do not seem to know it) of its limitations and dangers. Like the Sufis, the more advanced Zen Buddhists use the Heart center. They use it in walking practice and meditation. So it is always beneficial to practice a silence before effort—walking, gymnastics, dancing or anything—and to feel the breath. First one learns the ways of breathing and then one may practice the centering.

Some of these practices are found in the book, *Zen Flesh, Zen*

Bones [by Nyogen Senzaki and Paul Reps]. Many of the practices emphasize Heart-centering. Nevertheless, it is advantageous to practice the muscular Hara, to integrate the Body as well as the personality. This can first be done by either walking in the presence of a teacher or by following the examples set forth by a teacher.

8. The Use of Centers-II

If we study the lives of dancers, especially in this modern age since centering has been discovered, we can see its advantages and disadvantages. Isadora Duncan discovered the Hara center and used it. She did not have a teacher; she used it and unwisely abused herself, becoming more emotionally unstable and uncertain. Her life reflected her dancing and her dancing her life.

At the opposite end was the great Nijinsky who used the head centers. He could almost levitate. He rose from the denseness of the earth. His Body became ethereal, and at the same time his mind became ethereal. Like Isadora Duncan he was unbalanced, but in the opposite direction.

It is unwise to practice with the centers in the head for the purpose of Spiritual Walk until one has practiced with at least the Hara center. This gives balance. Sufism constantly emphasizes balance, but mentally-minded people often think if they have the words and thoughts, they have something. They have nothing until they are able to control centers and not be controlled by them. Besides, knowledge of breath is important, it may even be more important than centering.

Centering has a glamour which breathing does not, yet breathing is fundamental to life. We cannot live without it. So the pupil should certainly practice Hara; when the hold of Hara is very great, under wise guidance head-centering may be tried. But if not, then Heart-centering. The Heart center is near the center of the Body, and also in the unseen it is near the center of the personality.

In addition, certain attributes and qualities physically manifest through certain organs. If this were not so, the animal world would not have advanced, for in the lower creatures all functions are found in minuscule in all the cells. Differentiation, evolution and advancement all go together.

This would suggest that there is a centering in abdomen, a centering in head and a centering in thorax near heart—each with its purpose. As most people are weak they have to begin with Hara. After they are strong, they can practice Heart-centering with no end to advantage.

Head centering is mostly needed to increase Joy, Bliss, Lightness, rising above the denseness of the earth and material-mindedness. One should not, however, become the slave of it; one is not more "spiritual" just because one becomes more ethereal.

9. The Feet

When we become concerned with centers, we are likely to suppose that some parts of the Body are more to be venerated than others. There is a lesson in the First Epistle to the Corinthians in the Christian Bible to the contrary. Unfortunately, Christianity as a religion has not taught much about the nobility of the body, that the body is the temple of the divine spirit. It has become part of the Sufi Message to emphasize this.

No doubt it is easier to impress people with Abdomen-centering, Heart-centering and Head-centering. But Sufis have always been taught to watch their feet, and to feel that they are treading on God's earth.

There are breathing and other practices by which one learns to feel the magnetism go in and out through the feet. These practices can first be tried sitting, perhaps best with only the heels touching the ground. Then one can feel the magnetism while standing and afterwards while walking. One can concentrate on the feet.

The Japanese, concentrating on the abdomen, rid their minds of useless luggage. The Sufi dervishes use their feet, and also rid their minds of useless luggage. The ridding of luggage is more important than the method. What is needed is a method that works, not a philosophy about a method, which can be very confusing.

As one feels the breath go out the feet, this also helps one to overcome fatigue, as well as feel courage and direction. This practice also impels the breath to be felt through the whole Body. Then the Body acts as one. One has a whole Body, and the whole Body is the divine temple.

Again it has been taught that the last shall be first. We may begin with the head; we end with the feet. Each can produce the sense of oneness and this sense of oneness is most important in every school of spiritual development.

10. Tassawuri

Tassawuri is an advanced practice which requires a teacher, usually a living teacher. One does best by performing Tassawuri either in the presence of a living teacher, or when one has a firm impression of the teacher in the mind, it can be done in the teacher's absence. Or when the teacher manifests and brings a great blessing, Tassawuri can be performed easily.

There are several ways of acquiring Tassawuri. One is to see the teacher and even follow the teacher while walking. Another is to be deeply impressed, so that one is aware of the teacher's rhythm.

There are practices in concentration called <u>Murakkaba</u> which enable the devotee to advance along this line. Practices mean practices and not thoughts about such subjects. These thoughts are often the gates to the worst kind of delusions and self-centeredness. People may have the philosophies but neither the knowledge nor the wisdom. They do not know if they really can get into the rhythm of the teacher.

Sufic concentration (Murakkaba) requires devotion. Love, devotion and attunement are the best requirements. Then one feels, sometimes even sees the teacher, so to speak, without any physical contact. So one usually starts with the living teacher. But at the same time, the teacher may not be perfect and in turn may be practicing the rhythms of Rama, Krishna, Shiva, Buddha, Moses, Jesus, Mohammed or other illuminated souls.

Besides those named there have been a multitude of saints and some of these have been particularly respected. And others may manifest or impress their vibration upon a devotee. A devotee may need a particular kind of attunement to awaken certain qualities within. No better way can be used than the proper concentration and breath attunement followed by the practice of Spiritual Walk.

There is another form of Tassawuri used in the circumambulation of shrines. This has reached its highest degree in walking about the Kaaba at Mecca with the practice of Tassawuri Mohammed. This no doubt is the highest, hardest and also most rewarding practice. But being highest and hardest, it is like walking up a steep cliff, and it is better to learn to walk first, then climb slopes. Besides, the objective is to reach the summit, not necessarily to climb in a certain manner, for all ways lead to God.

Once one learns the principle, then it can be applied in all kinds of ways. There is yet another practice called Akhlak Allah which is to feel God, that one is in God's presence, that one is walking within God and God is walking within one. This is most beneficial and every body can learn to do that.

from "Spiritual Dancing" (1940)
Movement in Stillness, Stillness in Movement

by Murshid Samuel L. Lewis

The general laws of mechanics have been formulated by such great scientists as Newton and Avogadro, modified by Einstein and Planck in accordance with the discoveries made in laboratory and field, and corrected or adjusted to current mathematical knowledge. One finds a more or less unconscious conclusion in them that the natural motion of a body is in a straight line, and that these bodies, if unaffected, will move with constant <u>uniform acceleration</u>. That is to say, the <u>increase in speed</u> will be definite for each unit of superimposed time. The law of circular movement differs from this in that a body fixed upon such a path will continue onward with <u>uniform velocity</u> in that path. So even at first glance, the behavior of linear and circular movement is not the same. They seem to follow different laws, whereas a mathematical analysis reveals that they have merely adapted separate patterns.

There are two points here which a philosopher might note. While these laws or discoveries may be true, are they limited to an objective, physical world? May they not also apply to worlds unseen and undiscovered? Worlds unseen may be "physical" or not. Infra-red and ultra-violet rays are employed in photographic processes, and research using the electron microscope has added much to the human knowledge of what is "physical." For this reason, we may ignore differences, arbitrary or not, between physical, mental and spiritual. We may hold that truth is universal, and that laws which discovered to operate in one realm may also apply elsewhere. It may even be that thought and love are refined activities resembling, in their own ways, light and radiant energy.

The straight line was long upheld as the norm for activity and dynamic behavior. Ever since Euclid proclaimed the majesty of the straight line, the world has been dominated by masculine thought, masculine activity, masculine education and masculine ideas—more or less unconsciously. Perhaps some master psychologist or some disciple of Spengler will find the same secret, underlying motive in the contemporary revolt against Euclidean conventions with the rise of feminism in politics and social affairs. The masculine tendency is toward the straight line and flat plane, and man lives in a common sense world of three dimensions. But the feminine universe is composed of points and curves, and woman's space is of four dimensions.

To understand the spiritual and psychological aspects of art and life, we must study each of these in their proper setting and free ourselves from their dominance. What is spiritual synthesizes opposites, so it is said by the Sufi sage Hazrat Inayat Khan that God has no opposite.

China, ever old and ever young, has been a repository of wisdom and civilization. The Chinese would say that the universe is the result and interplay of two tremendous forces which they call Yin and Yang, the symbol of which is familiar to many who know not their meaning. Yin, it may be said, is the receptive or feminine aspect of life; Yang, the positive or masculine aspect. Yin is responsive and Yang expressive; Yin is beautiful and Yang is powerful. Yang is light and Yin is dark; Yang is activity and Yin repose or respite; Yang is expansion and Yin contraction. Light, the phenomenon of cosmic vibration is Yang; sound, the phenomenon of material atoms, is Yin. Yet there is no Yin completely devoid of

Yang or Yang completely devoid of Yin, except where destruction impends.

In other lands there have been parallel terms. Thus we read in the Bible of the pillars of the temple of Solomon, which the Free-Masons consider so important. One was called Jachin, almost identical with Yin; the other, Boas, the cognate of Yang. The Sufis speak of Jemal and Jelal. Yin is very close to, without being identical to, the Hindu prakriti. Yang has close correlations with the Hindu purusha.

In the mineral world, Yang dominates in all crystalline formations, whether metallic, non-metallic or compound. Yin, on the other hand, is in the natural glasses such as obsidian, which may be called the queen of the petrosphere. It is also in amorphous substances. This has led to one conception that Yang represents order and Yin disorder; that Yang dominates in the rational and Yin in the impulsive. But this conclusion overstresses one aspect which leads to masculinity instead of to balance. Balance is required more than anything else to reach perfection.

Again, we find that a crystal bowl has sharp edges, but a glass one is smooth and "soft." The Chinese knew this, and applied it in ceramics. Yin is in clay and Yang is in sand. From the former came porcelain, from the latter, glass. Fire is of the nature of Yang and adds Yang to Yin. In the formation of artificial glass, the fire is quickly quenched and thus Yang is withdrawn, so it is replaced by Yin. So here and there we find a dance, even in the world of rocky substances.

Yin is in clay and Yang is in sand, so these principles appear in the soil and in the vegetation which grows therefrom. Yin dominates in plants that grow in the water, for Yin and water are closely allied. Yang manifests in serophytic societies, the dwellers of desert, tundra and dry plain whose thorns and thickets attest to their nature. Yang is in the tall trees, Yin in the tendrils. Yang increases with calcium absorption and heat, and is noticeable in sugars and cellulose. Yin increases with sodium absorption and moisture and is also found in the starches. So it is throughout the universe—with beauty and pliability comes Yin, with strength and determination comes Yang.

Advancing to the animal world, we find Yang in shell, scale and bone as well as in the cell wall. Yin is in muscle, tendon, flesh and the cell interior. This is true also of the human body. But the human being is more than animal, for with humanity comes the ability to create as an artist. In the dance especially one uses the Body to express what one is or would be; this depends neither upon brush nor paint nor tool. In dance, the human artist uses what God has given, and with that can reproduce all the themes and thoughts of the infrahuman universe. For embellishment, he or she may add costume and scenery and may rely upon music as the greatest aid and asset. But underneath all, Yin and Yang will manifest in each effort and movement.

Static Symmetry corresponds to zero as a living number. Just as zero is a reality in statistics, graph representations and decimals, so static symmetry is a reality in the Spiritual Dance. It appears as the pause or rest in music, which so often accentuates a movement. In the dance, it is especially noticeable in what might be called vital or bionomic sculpture. Ancient friezes often depict an individual or an ensemble, and moderns rely upon them in their efforts to restore these forgotten methods. Through them the stone becomes flesh and Galatea [of the Greek myth] reincarnates anew.

Static Symmetry also appears in flower arrangement, that marvelous living art. Not so long ago, cut flowers were placed in vases or boxes or frames according to their size, color, variety and simple harmonies. The introduction of ichibana, the traditional Japanese system, has awakened something in the aesthetic spirit of man and has helped to revolutionize the decorative arts. Some Americans, notably Rudolph Schaeffer of San Francisco, have retained the spiritual philosophy of ichibana—the identity of life in artist and flower—while offering us an Occidental rather than Oriental art. He considers it better adapted to our personalities and more practical when applied to the growth of our gardens, fields and forests.

Another phase of Static Symmetry may be seen in animal training. Everyone who enjoys the circus or the vaudeville show has noticed how beasts are handled, both as individuals and in groups. When not performing, they may still be performing. The ensemble institutes a background, each animal being carefully educated to do his part and each finding a place in a graceful or symmetric pattern whether in doing its stunt or in waiting its turn. The background presents an excellent example of zero as a living number in art—repose as the basis of motion.

Statics is the science of bodies at rest. Even then, they are usually subject to many stresses and pulls. Lifeless forms depend upon mechanical centers of gravity. But a throbbing, vibrating, breathing, growing body may not always have an exact fixed point as such. Scientists say this is true even of the atom. Growth includes height (the Yang or Jelal factor) and girth (the Yin or Jemal factor). The increase of growth may be negative as well as positive, particularly with regards to girth. ("Girls, watch your waistline!") Changes in weight, too, affect the center of gravity.

The heart as static center may best be studied when the body is at rest, supine on the floor. To understand this better, let one take the position of the corpse and feel the heartbeat. Do not try at first to take any special position. Then lie flat on the back, stretching arms and feet to make the sign of the cross with the body. The "corpse" attests to involuntary, the cross to voluntary self-surrender, meaning, "I am nothing." The breath supplies its own rhythm and the heart begins to dance. The devotee may repeat sacred words while in that position; the dancer may listen to soothing music. The heart will throb and the inner light be augmented. This is the Alpha and the Omega of the spiritual dance, and to it one may always return.

After that, one should try lying on the left and on the right sides as if in sleep, preferably doing this without music, which might arouse discordant emotions and so distract one from the heart-concentration. After that, without turning attention from the heart, one may rest upon the bosom. Then one may dream. The mind here begins to assert itself. The vital forces are alert and the animal consciousness is aroused: one is awakening. Thus, there is relaxation and also stimulation. This is important: the tired dancer, snatching a few moments, will obtain knowledge common to the animals.

"Go to the ant, thou sluggard," said the wise Solomon. The ant has a well developed respiratory system which accounts both for its prowess (indicative of Yang operating through the breath) and intelligence (Yin operating through the breath). But this creature is not so advanced in the scale of heart, and according to the metaphysical Hindu classification would be regarded as a rakshasa (or raksha). Its circulatory system is by contrast quite undeveloped. Animals of flesh and blood which feed upon milk are more evolved in this respect. The cud-chewing cow, the cat basking in the sunlight, the horse in the meadow, have a far higher heart-knowledge which they reveal in their repose.

God, the Creator of the heavens and earth and of all the lower kingdoms of nature, made humanity in the divine image. So we may find something of the mineral, the plant and the animal in the human being. It is possible to assume "plant positions" and "animal positions"; these positions increase psychic power as well as animal and vital magnetism. The bird also contributed something in the course of evolution—the ability to stand erect. It is this characteristic, absorbed by the human being, which has earned us the name of anthropos, the upright one. To stand erect is part of the teaching of hygiene and choreography, and it need not be repeated here. But to keep the center of movement and feeling in or near the heart is most important, often neglected and shall be constantly reiterated.

The bird stands in relaxation and sleep but is not ungraceful. Its head may be lowered or turned to either side, while the eyes remain open or closed. There is a dance of the head known to the Muslims and further developed by the Sufi dervishes. It is helpful in memory training, though this has not been studied in the West. Its healing value is also great, rendering unnecessary some of the most delicate cervical adjustments. But humanity can learn more than this from the birds; we may rest like the swan, dove, eagle, robin or canary. We may observe them, concentrate upon them and portray them in the dance as well as in graphic or plastic art. Then we will be practicing static and dynamic eurhythmics, which will awaken in the mind a power of inspiration of which we have seldom dreamed. For simple is the alphabet of Terpsichore.

The prayerful head is held erect in praise and lowered in humility. Moving the head up and down and from side to side benefits the eyesight and aids the mind and nerves. In Static Symmetry, one studies each position separately and learns through intuition and practice. Head up, head down, head to the right, head to the left, relaxed position, then taut position—each has its own connotation.

Thus, we may call the model a dancer who emphasizes Static Symmetry. He or she can learn to hold each pose if heart-concentration is developed. Then one can relax with firmness, grace, power and beauty. Undertaken with such a concentration, this profession may add to the building of character.

In all standing positions, Yang predominates; in sitting posture there is more Yin. Sitting throws the weight from the feet (which are associated with Yang) to the base of the spine. Most people find it more comfortable and can remain seated far longer than they can stand. This relaxation brings repose to body and mind.

Kneeling is more common where the chair is not customary furniture. This posture brings one closer to earth and to nature and helps prevent loss of psychic energy. When the feet are not flat upon the floor or ground, they are "bioelectrically" not grounded or insulated. The breath is the channel for the vital force which we attract from space and also expel into space. If we are insulated, we preserve vitality and power. This adds to our health and wards off the perils of disease and age.

Hatha Yoga is a great science, especially necessary in a country like India, where because of climate and conditions, energetic athletic indulgence would be inadvisable. Yoga includes innumerable breathing exercises and postures, many of which could be learned by Westerners to their advantage. While some of these postures, or <u>asanas</u>, might be quite difficult for bony people without conferring much benefit upon them, there are others which can be learned.

It has to be understood that there are Yang bodies and Yin bodies. Yang bodies are bony and of two types: those with long backbones and legs, and those with strong skull and cheek formations. Yin bodies are also of two types: the ligamentous, and the vital or fleshy. The muscular type is balanced and stands midway between the others. Most Yoga postures are of the Yin type, and the people of India and the Malayan archipelago possess Yin bodies. But those of the Northeast of India, in whom the Aryan blood predominates, are of the Yang type. They have Yang bodies and they have been drawn to a Yang religion (Islam), of which the prayer movements are very beneficial for bony and mental people. So in India we find Yang people drawn to a Yang religion and Yin people drawn to a Yin religion, each with their respective attendant art forms.

Let us take into consideration the differences in physical form, without in any way advising against instruction in Hatha Yoga. A number of stances or positions are now presented which will give a better idea of the importance of Static Symmetry, the knowledge of which can only come through direct personal experience.

KNEELING WITH RECLINED THIGHS, BUTTOCKS ABOVE BACK OF FOOT: This is the devotee's position. "To God every head shall bow and knee shall bend" say the Hebrew Scriptures. This position signifies surrender of body and mind to God in humility. It is the essential posture of the Roman Catholic Church, quite in harmony with the general teachings of Catholic Christianity.

Keeping the concentration upon the heart, the dancer who performs this practice generates spiritual power. This is important for the evolution of every soul. When the legs are crossed, psychic power is derived from spiritual power. Most people, in ignorance, derive their psychic energy from other and less holy sources, not knowing the psychic laws, and either suffer for it, or cause others to lack energy.

Both of these positions are associated with earth. Their practice enables one to perform movements with bent knees.

SITTING POSTURE, WITH ONE LEG UNDER BODY, TOUCHING OPPOSITE BUTTOCKS, AND THE OTHER LEG IN FRONT: This is derived from the "Lotus Asana" of the Yogis and is better fitted for Western people. There are naturally two such positions, but for meditation it is advisable to sit upon the right foot and keep the left leg in front. The hands should be in the lap, one inside the other or else clasped; or they can be placed upon the thighs. This posture fosters relaxation. Then, the vital energy flows from the heart and becomes the source of mental magnetism and psychic power. These flow through the whole personality bringing blessing and benefit. Thus one experiences the life eternal in the midst of manifestation.

KNEELING, HEAD TOUCHING GROUND OR FLOOR, HANDS ON EITHER SIDE, ALSO TOUCHING THE GROUND OR FLOOR: This is the position of humility. It is also a fine blood-wash for the brain. The blood surges into the skull, cleansing and purifying brain and glands, especially when the heart-concentration is maintained. There is no chance for thought, so the mind rests. This is used in the Islamic prayers.

There are other positions which may be studied and which are needed as essentials of technique in various dances. Here we consider only those positions which are basic insofar as the dance contributes to the spiritual life and so far as the dancer may discover in her or his art what others may find in their church. Every breath involves an electrical current, the nature of which has been little studied even by biophysicists. Professor and Madame Roerich and Madame David-Neel report that the Tibetans have considerable knowledge on this subject.

Those interested in psychic research and metaphysics have already made investigations into the nature of the aura and of ectoplasm. The latter is presented in the cinema as a reality but is ignored in the materialistically-minded academies. It is harmful to shut off investigation which might unloose prejudices; alas, this occurs even in democracies. Thus the body-temple remains as a mystery until humanity becomes more truthful to itself.

Like any electrical instrument, the body exudes energy around points. Fingertips and toes are areas of leakage. The eye, sensitive to light, also reacts to bioelectrical phenomena. In the middle of the nineteenth century, Reichenbach, an Austrian investigator, conducted a series of laboratory experiments in this field only to be derided, persecuted and branded as a charlatan. But a new day is dawning, a new generation has arisen, and the work in the bioelectrical nature of the Body will not go forever unheeded.

CHAPTER SEVEN

The Coming Universality

[The following is a formal esoteric commentary by Murshid Samuel L. Lewis (Sufi Ahmed Murad Chisti) on the work of his teacher Pir-O-Murshid Hazrat Inayat Khan. "GATHA" is the writing of Hazrat Inayat Khan (written between 1920-26); "TASSAWUF" (Sufi term for esoteric teaching) is the voice of Murshid Samuel L. Lewis (written between 1965-70). The following is excerpted from a series of papers on "Metaphysics."--ed.]

Gatha: When the nations will recognize the divine law and the law of the time, then humanity will no longer be ruled by the laws made by a few intellectual people for their convenience and as they think right, but the law will recognize the divine indication which is constantly working through every soul, guiding it on the path, showing it the way of destiny.

Tassawuf: This subject also appears in several places in the Sufi literature as in "The Eastern Rose Garden, "Alchemy of Happiness," etc. [writings of Hazrat Inayat Khan]. The difference between the true disciple and the crystalized devotee is that the true disciple may both see the growth and partake of it. As has been said, a described God is a dethroned God, so a described and fixated evolution is no evolution at all. Although India in particular has had some sages and seers, those who could perceive directly have often been the least capable of perceiving widely. Indeed, it may even be better to perceive widely. That is the nature of the heart.

If one really looks, most of the rising protests are efforts of the

If one really looks, most of the rising protests are efforts of the soul of humanity toward freedom, compassion, and love.

Gatha: And when such a time will come, there will not be a necessity for so many laws, and as many laws, so many lawyers, and probably as many lawyers, so many law courts, and no end of prisons and no limit to the prisoners. This will cease to exist. There will not be the necessity for strict laws and severe punishments for nothing.

Tassawuf: It is both remarkable and amusing that persons who have reacted to the real or imaginary persecution of early Christians and later of witches, have made so many acts of human beings criminal which aren't only not against the Mosaic Code but not against any teachings of Jesus. On the contrary, many so-called law breakers often believe both in the spirit and form of the Sermon on the Mount while the so-called law preservers have no such outlook. This means in the end they will be overthrown. While God cannot be said to be for or against any political party or outlook, God certainly deserves basic human freedom. Besides this, the Bible teaches that God brought forth trees and herbs for the good of human kind. From the spiritual point of view it is almost impossible to conceive that those who have discovered usages or pleasures from the many trees and herbs have been condemned as criminals. This condition will not, cannot, last.

Gatha: If one could only see that among 100 people who are sentenced by the courts, there is hardly one to be blamed, to be held responsible for his faults. And if there is anyone to be held responsible, it is all we human beings. Why do we not all work? Why do we not all help them to kindle the light in their soul that would show their path plainly?

Tassawuf: In the generations between the giving of the Message and this commentary, there has been a rising recognition of this. Much is blamed on 'environment.' The meaning of this word is not clear. But it is better to blame environment than to blame individuals. This all belongs to samsara [the impressions of the reactive mind] and will lead sooner or later to a deeper study of mystical and spiritual teachings.

Gatha: It is not necessary that the clergyman, the priest only should be responsible for the evolution of each individual. We all must work in the capacity of brother and sister to everyone. In the realization of the human family in the Parenthood of God, we must hold it as our duty, our sacred task, to waken in our brothers and sisters, with love, with respect, with modesty, with humility, that power of understanding what is really for their best, which can really benefit them.

Tassawuf: In the ensuing years there has been the rise of the science of sociology which strives to see life as a whole. We can almost call it the study of samsara from the materialistic side. This is a beginning. It will help because those involved who have to face so much misfortune, so much pain, so many shortcomings in their clients, begin to awaken sympathy in their hearts. This is a grand step forward.

The other is in the evolution of humanity itself as has been explained. This is invariably toward greater heart outlooks.

Gatha: It is not the mission of one person, it is the mission of every person. And if we each considered our share of the work in the Message and showed it by our own example in the world, we should be doing a great duty toward God and humanity.

Tassawuf: When the Message was first given the immediate hearers began to regard themselves as a privileged aristocracy. But the same was true in many other modern establishments who verbalized or thought or felt the broader outlooks. But in this first stage there was either competition or non-recognition. Too many world brotherhoods with big brothers. The modern Message of Sufism is that the Brotherhood, the Human Family, will form of itself. This stressing of particular persons or movements or philosophies shows the absence of modesty and often the absence of evolved morality. But the high morality issues from the soul itself, and we will be seeing a greater and grander growth and mutual recognition until humanity will rise up and demand—No More War.

II. BEGINNING TO DANCE
(INCLUDING INSTRUCTIONS TO
DANCES OF UNIVERSAL PEACE, VOLUME I)

How to Dance—11 Keys

Here are some keys which will help the dancing be more meaningful for you. To do even one or two of these will have a profound effect:

1. LISTEN. Do not simply recite the sacred phrase. Listen to the other voices. Listen to the person directing the dance. When you begin to listen, your voice will automatically begin to harmonize. Find the center of the sound.

2. FEEL. The dances are designed to take us more and more into the universe of feeling. Stay with your feeling. If you go off into the world of thoughts, don't judge yourself; simply bring your concentration back to feeling. The heart center, found in the middle of the chest, is the natural place to begin.

3. CONCENTRATE ON THE SACRED PHRASE. The sacred phrase, sometimes referred to as Wazifa or Mantra, centers the dance. We all say this together. The Grace of Allah can operate through the sacred phrase if we are willing to receive it, to let it be. With each repetition feel the phrase touching your being in a deeper and deeper way.

4. DON'T BE AFRAID TO STOP THE DANCE. This is for the dance leaders. If the dance gets out of control, or just isn't making it, it is much better to stop and begin anew. Learning is much more important than just doing.

5. SIMPLE, RHYTHMIC MUSIC. This can be a great aid. Guitar and drum are especially helpful. Musicians should emphatically resist

going off on their own. The sacred phrase must be uppermost in their concentration. The music should accentuate the natural rhythm of the sacred phrase. Drummers especially bear this in mind. The simpler the better. Don't dominate the space. The sacred phrase should by far be the loudest sound. If you play your instrument correctly, no one will even notice you. Isn't that wonderful?

6. MOVE TOGETHER. Restrain the exuberant impulse to make an individual expression. You will be amazed how much higher/deeper the dances are when you use that same energy to harmonize with the others in the circle. Feel your body fully. Then gradually or suddenly become the whole circle.

7. WATCH YOUR BREATH. Breath is life. Breath is movement. Voice is breath. Let breath breathe. Return to awareness of breath in silence between dances. Notice the subtle changes in breath brought about by each dance.

8. ECSTASY. These dances can lead to states of ecstasy. Joyously invigorating! In dances where you are brought to the center of the circle, especially soar. But soar with your whole being. Taste all planes at the same time. If your feet are grounded on the earth then your head can be in the heavens.

9. DEVOTION. This is a grace. To willingly submit ourselves to Allah/God in Whom we live and move and have our being. Hypocrisy may be the only sin. How wonderful it is when we actually feel like bowing in humility before the eternal truth. These dances can be worship: the celebration of the Divine Presence. The Sufis call this Akhlak Allah—acting as if in the Presence of Allah; and knowing that even if you don't see Allah, verily Allah sees you.

10. AMIN (ah-meen). This means "so be it." We say this at the

conclusion of many dances. (Other phrases such as the Sanskrit "Svaha" are also used). The important thing is not to say it, but to mean it, to affirm with one's whole being.

11. SILENCE. There may be a silent meditation before the dance starts but if the participants are not experienced in this they may learn the meditation through dancing and also learn the dancing through meditation. As the sound and music of the dance stop, enter the silence. This is your opportunity to hear what has been created. In this silence one can absorb the qualities evoked during the dance. This is the most important part of the dance. It becomes all-encompassing.

Beloved Ones of Allah, all these words are in hope of your falling awake and finding the truth in your own self. You know your own experience better than anyone else. Be true to that. Don't let anyone pull the wool over your eyes; neither be swayed from what you know by the opinions of others. Always be willing to learn. When asked what was the secret of his success, Murshid Samuel Lewis said, "Big ears!"

—Wali Ali Meyer, 1988

THE MUSIC OF THE EARLY
DANCES AND SONGS

When the Sufi Choir first formed in 1969, Murshid Samuel L. Lewis would stand in the bass section singing loud, clear and out of tune. By normal musical standards Murshid's singing was marginal. But the music in him led others toward a magnificent musical vision. By his own example he showed us how perfection of the heart opens the way to a higher musical ecstasy. On the occasions when he would lead the singing he would hop about like Krishna, singing each part in a strong if nasal bass, whipping the singers into the song with dervish energy.

It is true that music must be sung in tune and in time. But music so made does not always bridge heaven and earth. A certain initiation occurs when one suddenly sees that music can be out of tune and out of time, but still carry a powerful spirit. The pedagogy of musical technique is well known by a million teachers. But the methodical development of the heart and the techniques expressing the heart's refinement are not so obvious. Pir-O-Murshid Hazrat Inayat Khan was the first to formulate this in the West; Murshid Samuel Lewis (his disciple) and Pir Vilayat (his son) have deepened these teachings by redefining them in the present.

There is an eternal aspect to every sound, and it is this enduring quality to which the open heart tunes. When a musician has also mastered pitch and time, the results are sublime and the integrative ideal is touched. It is a matter of emphasis. If you study musical technique, the heart may or may not open; but if the heart is opened, technique will come to give it wings.

This is Murshid's teaching. It seems to awaken something in Americans that has been asleep. Living teachers who transmit this by their presence are rare, but there. If you are ready to find one, you will. The music for the Dances of Universal Peace and the Sufi

Choir came from this transmission, both in its composition and in its expression. So forcefully have the dances and songs channeled through those who danced in Murshid's footsteps that one can see the making of a tradition, the forming of a river. The source is the purity of heart which arises from concentration on the Divine Attributes.

The river is swelling, not only in the West. All over the world people are gathering together to sing with their voices and their hearts in tune—more now than ever. The purpose of this music is to facilitate this gathering.

—Notes by William Allaudin Mathieu, 1975
Director of the Sufi Choir

NOTES FOR DANCE MUSICIANS

It is very helpful to have a drummer and/or a guitarist accompanying the dancing. If at all possible they should be trained in both the inner and outer dimensions of the dances. Here are suggestions from some experienced teachers:

Having a guitar or some other tonal instrument is of great benefit to most dances, adding one more element of unity to the experience. For guitarists, the most convenient tuning, or at least the one most widely used is:

Low E string up to G; A down to G; D stays D; G stays G; B down to G; E down to D. So, from lowest to highest: GGDGGD.

One then plays melodically in the key of G using a scale with a feeling or emotion according to the Dance. In the case where the most convenient key for the voice is C, one capos up to the fifth fret and so forth for other keys.

There are chords that can be found in this tuning, but first one should focus on learning the basic shape of scale that fits the sacred phrase. In melodic dances this is defined. In chanted or "two-note" dances, the guitarist must breathe with the sacred phrase and with the leader and find a melodic shape that stems from this attunement.

It is not important to play all of the strings all the time. Guitarists should attune carefully to the dance leader and be aware of the changes in energy: loud, soft, expansive, receptive, bright, reflective. By breathing with and singing the sacred phrase, these all come to the fingers by grace, without thought. Let the feeling that "I" am playing music go, and let the "I am"—the Oneness—do it.

The drum is a symbol of the living heart, and the drummer especially of all the musicians provides the heartbeat for the dance. Drummers should be experienced in the dance, so that they can notice where the lead foot falls: this should normally correspond with the "doum" or deepest tone of the instrument. Excellent drummers can keep the basic beat, so that the dancers' feet always feel where to go, while still modifying their stroke, touch and feeling for each different sacred phrase used in the dance. This comes with time; again the key is to concentrate on the sacred phrases which the dancers are repeating.

The musicians must be attuned as well as in tune. The drummers must watch the leader of the dance, yet be positive enough to keep a strong rhythm. As the drummer is used to following the leader, the leader is in turn relying on the steadiness of the rhythm for the dance. If the drummer is always being receptive or following, the rhythm fluctuates, instead of remaining steady. On the other hand, if the leader wants to alter the tempo of the dance, the musicians must be right there.

Technique aside, it is the heart-concentration which enables this steadiness with flexibility in dance musicians. For this reason, new musicians who wish to join in should be instructed to first dance, feel the sacred phrase in their bodies, and then gradually find their way to being of service in the circle of musicians. A musician who cannot express the sacred phrase in movement will not be able to express it in his or her playing.

—Excerpted from the Teachers Dance Manual with additions
by Saadi Neil Douglas-Klotz

INTRODUCTORY BISMILLAH
(Key of G, open tuning)

1. Allah (repeat 10 times)   (literally, the "Oneness")
2. Er Rahman, Er Rahim   (Divine attributes of mercy and compassion)
3. Allah, Allah,
   Allah, Allah

Often the first dance performed in a meeting, this is also one of the first dances presented by Murshid Samuel Lewis. It is named "Introductory" because other more complex "Bismillah" dances followed. Rahman and Rahim are both derived from the Arabic root <u>rahm</u>, meaning "womb, the birth of divine love into the world." The meeting may be opened with all joining hands in a circle (or concentric circles) and reciting the Sufi Invocation given by Hazrat Inayat Khan:

Toward the One, the Perfection of Love,
Harmony and Beauty, the Only Being,
United with all the Illuminated Souls
Who form the Embodiment of the Master,
The Spirit of Guidance.

The group may also recite the following invocation in Arabic: <u>Bismillah-er-Rahman er-Rahim</u>. We begin in the name of Allah, most merciful and compassionate. Or: With the light of the One, from whom is born mercy and compassion. Any translation is only approximate, but it is better if the group knows what it is saying, and says it with devotion, than if it merely recites a formula because it is customary.

The meeting may also be opened with a practice or concentration that communicates the same intention and unifies the group experience. (For example, all walking and breathing the phrase "Toward the One" with an awareness of the heart center.)

1. All join hands in a circle and move to the right, starting on the right foot, while chanting "Allah" ten times.

2. Continuing to the right, raise joined hands on "Er Rahman" and lower arms on "Er Rahim."

3. Holding hands in a circle, move to right as in 1. Alternate movements 2. and 3. for a total of four repetitions.

After that, movement 2. may change to:

2. Half turn. All release hands, raise arms and make a half turn (180 degrees) on "Er Rahman," rejoining lowered hands on "Er Rahim."

During the next cycles of four, movement 2. may change to 'full turn,' 'turn-and-a-half,' 'two turns,' 'three turns'...

The dance ends with all spinning individually on "Er Rahman, Er Rahim."

The leader may vary this dance in a number of ways: by changing the number of turns in a balanced fashion, by emphasizing the group breath, by alternating singing and silence or otherwise. However, it is important to have a firm foundation in the original sequence before changing it. In using any variation, one should be mindful of the overall intention of the dance.

As-Salaam Aleikum Greeting Dance

(For partners, Key of G or C, open tuning)

1. As-salaam aleikum   (Peace be with you)
   As-salaam aleikum
   As-salaam aleikum
2. La illaha el il Allah   (There is no God but God)

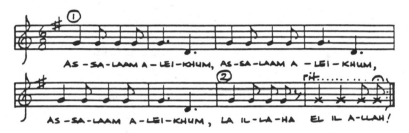

An original Dance of Murshid Samuel Lewis.

"As-salaam aleikum" is a traditional Islamic greeting, asking that the full blessing and experience of peace be with the one greeted. "La illaha el il Allah" is a phrase of <u>zikr</u>, or "remembrance." This form is rendered in an Egyptian dialect of Arabic that Murshid Samuel Lewis encountered on a trip to Egypt in 1960-61 and then used in this Dance.

All take partners. Dancers will progress past each partner to a new partner in the direction they now face in the circle.

1. Partners join hands with each other and circle clockwise, raising arms on "As-salaam alei-" and lowering on "-kum," while bowing slightly.

2. Spin individually with arms raised, while progressing to the next partner. On "Allah," bow to new partner with hands held in prayer mudra (palm to palm) at the heart.

Dance begins again.

ALHAMDULLILAH ROUND DANCE
(Key of C, standard tuning)

1. Alhamdulillah, Alhamdulillah,
2. Alhamdulillah.
3. Alhamdulillah, Alhamdulillah,
4. Alhamdulillah.

Chorus:
5. Praise the Lord, Praise the Lord,
   Praise the Lord, Praise the Lord.

This Arabic phrase translates to "All praise belongs to Allah. Everything praiseworthy comes from and returns to the One." One of Murshid S.A.M.'s close friends, Shemseddin Ahmed, offered as a further translation that "each being has a unique hamd or quality which is to be brought into manifestation and action for the benefit of all and for the praise of Allah."

This song may be done as a dance in unison or as a four-part round. If numbers permit four concentric circles, the dance may also be done as a round.

Dance: Form a circle, drop hands and face right (all facing the line of direction). The circle will move in a counterclockwise direction.

1. All walk forward in the line of direction. On each repetition of "Alhamdulillah" throughout the dance, the hands touch the heart and are then raised up and out above the head in a gesture of praise.

2. Spin to the right with the hand movement.

3. Face the center of the circle and sidestep to the right with the hand movement for each repetition.

4. Spin to the right with the hand movement, ending up facing the line of direction (or facing the center of the circle for the chorus).

Repeat 1 thru 4 at least once more before going on to:

5. Chorus: With arms around each other (closer together than 'hands on shoulders'), step to the right. This is repeated once more or as often as the leader feels appropriate. The dance may also be done without this chorus for a simpler version.

Dance begins again.

Round: This is a beautiful and joyful four-part round. Although four mixed groups can sing this, the chorus (Praise the Lord) sounds best with two groups of women (soprano and alto) and two groups of men (tenor and bass). It sounds full without instrumental accompaniment or it may have guitar, drum or other instruments.

Everyone must pay attention for the place where the leader brings in the chorus. Certain singers will have to interrupt their "Alhamdulillah" in mid-word. The leader gives the "Praise the Lord" cue when the round reaches its peak.

If this round is done as a dance, the group must first learn the round so there is a clear understanding of the round entrances (1.,2.,3.,4.). The leader may vary the complexity of this dance according to the group; i.e. a two-circle round without the chorus.

As-Salaam Aleikum Duet
(Key of C)

(Traditional Islamic greeting: May peace be with you.)

1. As-salaam aleikum   (Peace be with you)
   As-salaam aleikum
   As-salaam aleikum
   La illaha el il Allah   (There is no God but God)

Divide into two groups (men and women or mixed). Everyone sings the first and second line in unison. Then the first group sings the first line as the second group sings the second line, alternating lines as the song continues. End with everyone singing "Hu."

This is an enjoyable practice for couples and may even lend itself to a simple dance. At first the song may take some concentrated practice (it's not especially easy to sing), but if one focuses on the feeling of the phrase and the beauty of the music, the sense of greeting may expand from the personal to universal.

DIVINE ATTRIBUTE WALKS
(Key of C or G, open tuning)

The following is a sample of the Divine Attribute Walks. This practice of Sifat-i-Allah (the ninety-nine names or qualities of Allah) offers each person the opportunity to manifest divine qualities by combining feeling, movement and recitation of the sacred phrase in what may be considered a meditation in action.

These Walks are usually done with all facing counterclockwise in a circle. The leader may introduce and demonstrate the movement for each attribute, or, as Samuel Lewis did, ask each participant to feel the sacred phrase deeply and move from this feeling. If a movement is demonstrated, the walkers follow this movement, harmonize their voices and, above all else, feel how that quality arises from their own being. It is helpful for the leader to mention the English translation for each phrase.

Ya Hayyoo, Ya Qayoom (O Ever-Living, O Eternal) Arms are raised up and out above the head on "Ya Hayyoo"; the palms are brought together in front of the heart on "Ya," then the palms are brought down and spread out to both sides at waist level on"Qayoom."

Ya Azim (O Thou Most High!) Arms are raised and held high above the head, reaching straight up as far as possible. Allah is beyond the mind.

Ya Fattah (O Opener of the Way) The "ah" sound is emphasized. Hands touch the heart, then open wide in a rapid movement on the"-tah." Allah is the remover of all obstacles and difficulties.

WAZIFA CANON

(Key of D or C, open tuning)

1. La illaha   (There is none)
2. Il Allah Hu   (except the One)
   (Repeat 3 times)
3. Ishk Allah Mahbud Lillah   (Love, lover and
   Ishk Allah Mahbud Lillah   beloved are One)
4. Ya Rahman   (The compassionate)
5. Ya Rahim   (The merciful)
6. Il Allah Hu   (Only God is)
7. Subhan Allah   (God is pure)
8. Alhamdulillah   (All praise to God)
9. Allaho Akbar   (Peace is Power)
   (Repeat 3 times)

This is a three part canon and may also be done as a three part dance if there are enough dancers to form three concentric circles.

Three-Part Canon: All sing the entire melody in unison the first time. On the second repetition, the first group continues with the melody (line 3.) as the second and third group sing an extra repetition of 1. and 2.—"La illaha il Allah Hu." Then the second group continues with the melody (line 3.) as the third group sings an additional repetition of "La illaha il Allah Hu" before continuing on to the rest of the melody.

This canon is unusual in that at one point all three parts are singing the same notes (on the "Allaho Akbar"). If the singing peaks at this point, there is an added effect. This dance or canon ends beautifully with all repeating "La illaha il Allah Hu" a number of times.

Dance:
1. All hold hands in a circle and step backward while slightly bowing, concentrating on the emptiness of limitation or division.

2. All step toward the center of the circle, raising joined hands, concentrating on the fullness of unity and perfection; the all-inclusiveness of Divine Unity.

Repeat 1 and 2 for a total of three times (or as canon directions above for three circles).

3. Dancers place right hand over the heart of the person to their right. Their left hand covers the hand that is on their heart. All step to the right. (Alternate movement: Each person places their hands on the back—opposite the heart—of person to either side.)

4. All turn right to face the line of direction, counterclockwise, and walk with arms extended, palms down.

5. Continue to walk in the line of direction with arms extended, palms up.

6. Spin to the right, in place, and end up facing the center of the

circle with the hands held palm to palm at the heart on "Hu."

7. Walk in the line of direction with hands cupped, one on top of the other, at waist level.

8. Continue to walk in the line of direction. Both hands touch the heart and are raised up and out above the head in the gesture of praise.

9. All face the center of the circle with hands firmly on the shoulders of those to either side and step to the right.

Dance begins again. The Dance ends with a few repetitions of 1. and 2.

ALLAH-HO-AKBAR DUET
(Key of C)

If the conductor has a clear understanding of this rhythm, a group of mixed voices can achieve a full sound with this duet. It sounds best when conducted with a definite and positive rhythm. Pay special attention to the pitch of the last bass "F." The translation of this phrase is: "There is no power or might save in Allah" or "Peace is Power."

Ya Azim
(Key of G, open tuning)

1. Ya Azim, Ya Azim (O Thou, most High)
2. El Allah Hu, (Only Allah is)
   El Allah Hu
3. Allah Hu (The One who is)
4. Alleluia (Praise to the One)

This three-part round may also be done as a three-circle dance if there are enough dancers to form three concentric circles. For best musical results when performed as a round, divide the women into higher and lower voices and have all the men sing in unison. Round entrances are marked in the music with a star. The syncopated rhythm is crisp and must be understood by the singers. The unstruck downbeat of the third bar must be heard as an unstruck downbeat. Only in this way will the ensemble rhythm be clear.

1. All face right and walk in the line of direction, counterclockwise, with the arms raised high above the head.
2. All face the center of the circle, join hands and continue moving to the right.
3. Raise joined hands.
4. Spin in place, clockwise (toward the right hand).
Dance begins again.

Alternate Version: (for partners)

Take partners. Dancers will progress past their partner to a new partner in the direction they now face in the circle.

1. Partners join hands with each other and circle clockwise, with hands lowered on "Ya" and raised high on "Azim."

2. Spin individually, first to the right and then to the left.

3. With the hands held palm to palm at the heart, partners face each other and bow on "Hu."

4. Spin individually and progress to new partner.

Dance begins again.

YA HAYY YA HAQQ
(Key of G, open tuning)

1. Ya Hayy Ya Haqq (four times) (O Life, O Truth)
2. Ya Hayy Ya Haqq (four times)
3. Ya Hayy Ya Haqq (four times)
4. Ya Hayy Ya Haqq (four times)

This is one of Murshid Samuel Lewis' original dances, invoking the divine attributes of Life and Truth. "Hayy" refers to the life energy which energizes the cosmos. "Haqq" is the truth which comes when this life force is embodied—it is what each being can make real of the Divine Reality. It is a simple yet powerful dance.

The circle moves in a counterclockwise direction throughout the dance. Rhythm is very important, and the drummer should hold a steady drum beat throughout, resisting the impetus of this dance to speed up.

The phrase is repeated four times for each movement. Each repetition is given eight beats (four for "Ya Hayy" and four for "Ya Haqq"). Throughout the dance, the arms are raised on "Ya Hayy" and lowered on "Ya Haqq."

1. Walk in the line of direction.
2. Turn in place.
3. Face the center of the circle and sidestep to the right. The arms are extended toward the center of the circle on "Ya Hayy" and lowered on "Ya Haqq."
4. All join hands and raise arms on "Ya Hayy" and lower on "Ya Haqq" while sidestepping to the right.

Dancers release hands and face the line of direction as the dance begins again. After two or three cycles, the leader may call for double time; two beats for "Ya Hayy" and two beats for "Ya Haqq." The tempo may again be doubled to one beat for each phrase.

The dance may be allowed to build slowly. What is essential is that dancers feel the difference of quality between the two phrases, and that they let the sacred phrases "do them" rather than forcing things with ego will-power.

To conclude, all stand in place with arms raised for an extended "Ya Hayy" and lowered on an emphatic "Ya Haqq."

'TIS A GIFT TO BE SIMPLE
(Key of C, open or standard tuning)

1. 'Tis a gift to be simple, 'Tis a gift to be free,
2. 'Tis a gift to come down where we want to be,
3. And when we have come down to the place just right,
    We will be in the valley of
4. Love and delight.
5. When the true simplicity is gained,
6. To bow and to bend we shan't be ashamed.
7. To turn, to turn, t'will be our delight
    'til by turning and turning
8. We come 'round right.

This traditional Shaker song is a favorite of children, and it can serve to awaken the childlike nature in us all.

This dance is another of Murshid Samuel Lewis' originals. It may be led by demonstration without oral directions. The pause at the end of each cycle is important; it helps to maintain the unity and integrity of the group.

If sung with the counterpoint ("La illaha el il Allah Hu"), the guitarist should play in standard tuning. The syncopation in the counterpoint is essential for musical success.

1. All join hands in a circle and skip to the right.
2. All kneel, continuing to hold hands.
3. While kneeling, place hands on shoulders of those on either side and sway from side to side, beginning on the right side.
4. Place both hands over the heart on "love" and open arms wide on "delight."
5. All stand, join hands and skip to the right.
6. "Bow and bend" in rhythm with the music.
7. Spin individually to the right.
8. All move in toward the center of the circle with arms around

(arms around shoulders or waist of persons on both sides) and pause briefly.

Dance begins again.

TEMPLE SONG

(Key of C, open tuning)

1. This is not my Body.
2. This is the temple of God.
3. This is not my heart.
4. This is the altar of God.

This English phrase was given as an advanced concentration practice by Pir-O-Murshid Hazrat Inayat Khan. It expresses a certain state of the mystic in which one feels the divine acting through one. The Sufis describe this state as <u>fana</u>, divine effacement. The reciprocal state is called <u>baka</u>, or divine expression. Meister Eckhart expressed this in the statement, "I see now that the eyes through which I see God are the eyes through which God sees me."

This is a beautiful four-part round. Entrances are best made in the order of alto, tenor, soprano, and bass. Be careful to make a clear distinction between notes in the triplets even though they are quickly sung.

DERVISH BISMILLAH DANCE
(Key of C, open tuning)

1. Bismillah
   Er Rahman Er Rahim

   (In the name/light of Allah, who is mercy and compassion)

2. Allah, Allah,
   Allah, Allah

3. La illaha illa 'llah
   Ishk Allah Mahbud Lillah

   (There is no one but the One)
   (God is love, lover and beloved)

4. Bismillah
   Er Rahman Er Rahim

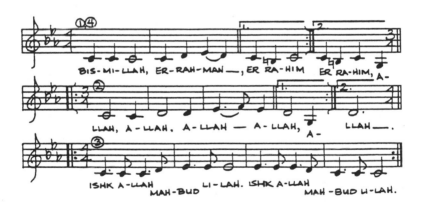

Another translation for "La illaha illa 'llah" is "There is no reality except in unity." This cycle of zikr (lit., remembrance) dances is derived from ceremonial movements of the Turkish Mevlevi Order of Dervishes.

With a group that has achieved some unity and attunement, it can be led with very little verbal direction.

1. All hold hands with fingers interlaced and sidestep to the

right for four repetitions of the phrase and to the left for four repetitions. This sequence may continue, or at the leader's discretion, all may come close together, shoulder to shoulder, and repeat the phrase eight times while swaying from side to side in place in rhythm with the leader. The leader raises his/her voice on the last phrase to indicate the close of the first cycle.

2. With hands joined, step backward from the center of the circle, chanting "Allah" four times, once with each step. Then all sidestep to the right while chanting "Allah" twelve times and to the left for sixteen more repetitions.

Continuing to the left, drop hands and face the line of direction. While taking one step forward with the right foot, the left arm is crossed over the chest with the left hand placed just below the right shoulder on the first "Allah." While taking a second step forward with the left foot, the right arm is crossed over the left arm on the second"Allah." Then make one full turn in place clockwise (to the right) while chanting the third and fourth"Allah." End up facing the line of direction (to the left) and lower the arms. Do this a total of four times. After the fourth repetition, end up facing the other direction (circle will now move in a counterclockwise direction).

All now walk to the right in the line of direction keeping arms crossed over the chest, right arm over the left. Take one step forward with the left foot and bow slightly toward the center of the circle on the first "Allah." Take one step forward with the right foot and bow slightly toward the outside on the next "Allah." Continue this until "Allah" has been chanted sixteen times. This concludes the second cycle of the dance.

3. The men form an inner circle by kneeling close together with hands joined, fingers interlaced, and chant the zikr phrase, "La illaha illa 'llah." The head swings in a circular motion, from the left shoulder to the right shoulder and then up on "La illaha." The head is lowered toward the heart on"illa" and raised on "'llah."

The women form an outer circle with arms on each other's shoulders and step to the right while singing "Ishk Allah Mahbud

Lillah" in rhythm with the men's chant: i.e. "Ishk Allah" with the "La illaha" and "Mahbud Lillah" with the "illa 'llah." This continues until the leader ends this cycle with "Amin." As a variation, the men and women may be directed to switch singing parts while continuing with their same movement.

4. All form one circle, holding hands with fingers interlaced. Stand close together with shoulders touching shoulders. In rhythm with the leader, all sway from side to side in place while chanting "Bismillah er Rahman er Rahim" twenty times. This starts slowly and builds in tempo until the 17th or18th repetition, then very deliberately slows for the last two or three repetitions. To end this cycle, the leader raises his or her voice on the final phrase. All maintain the same position for a few moments of full silence. Conclude with all bowing to the center of the circle with arms crossed, fingertips resting on shoulders, right arm over left. Amin.

Note: Throughout this dance, the leader may continue each cycle or phrase for as long or short as is felt appropriate.

DERVISH CHANTED ZIKR

On the recording, Murshid Wali Ali chants this powerful Sufi zikr ("remembrance") practice.

SAT NAM DANCE
(Key of C, open tuning)

1. Ek Ong Kar Sat Nam   (There is One God)
    Siri Wah (e) Guru   (Truth is God's Name)
    Repeat.   (Indescribable is God's Wisdom)
2. Siri Wah (e) Guruji
    Siri Wah (e) Guru
    Repeat.

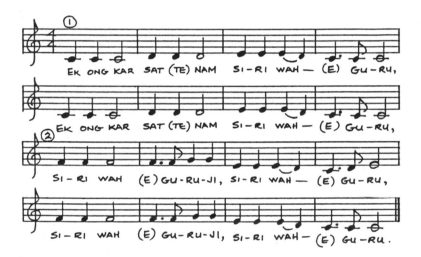

This phrase comes from the Sikh tradition. "Wah Guru" does not refer to a particular teacher, but to the teaching of the cosmos; Yogi Bhajan has translated this phrase as "the ecstasy of infinity."

All join hands in a circle.

First time through:

1. With hands joined, all step to the right during the first repetition and to the left on the second.

2. With the arms raised, spin individually to the right on the first repetition and to the left on the second.

Second time through:

1. With hands joined in a circle, swing arms together while moving to the right, then left.

2. Spin individually to the right and to the left.

Third time through:

1. Egyptian position: With elbows bent and forearms raised, place hands palm to palm (at ear level) with dancers on either side. The head is turned from side to side in rhythm.

2. Spin individually to the right and to the left.

Fourth time through:

1. Place hands on shoulders of dancers on either side and step to the right, then to the left.

2. Spin individually to the right and to the left.

Dance begins again. After the second or third cycle, the leader may increase the tempo. To conclude, a final verse may be done with arms around (closer together than hands on shoulders).

RAM NAM SNAKE DANCE
(Key of G or C, open tuning)

1. Om Sri Ram Jai Ram
    Jai Jai Ram

(God who at once is truth
and power, impersonal and
personal! Victory to Thee!
Victory,victory to Thee!)

OM SRI RAM JAI RAM JAI JAI RAM, OM SRI RAM JAI RAM JAI JAI RAM, OM

This mantra was received from Swami Papa Ramdas and Mother Krishnabai of Anandashram. Heard on the recording is Murshid Samuel Lewis leading this dance at a public meeting in California in 1970. His voice amply speaks for itself!

This is an example of a snake or line dance, with the leader at the head of the line of dancers. The dancers follow the leader; it is very effective if all move in harmony. The leader may weave the line in any pattern on the dance floor. It is wise to move forward slowly. This type of dance can become energetic, and it is important that the leader be aware of the entire line of dancers. The end of the line will have a tendency to exaggerate any twists, turns or speed of the line.

The leader calls out or demonstrates new movements for each few repetitions of the phrase. Although the basic form is one of holding hands and walking, many variations are possible: hands on the waist of the person in front; hands on shoulders; sidestepping; very little steps; and so on as the leader may invent. To "thread the needle," the leader doubles back on the line of dancers and weaves back and forth under the raised arms of every third or fourth person. It is important that all be moving forward slowly when this is done. The persons who have been 'woven under' will have to make a full turn in place as the line progresses.

The dance may end with the leader being 'caught' in the center of a spiral formation. End with all saying "Om Hari Om."

Another original dance of Murshid Samuel Lewis using this same chanted phrase and rhythm follows.

RAM NAM—CIRCLES OF FIVE
(Key of G or C, open tuning)

1. Om Sri Ram Jai Ram Jai Jai Ram
2. Om Sri Ram Jai Ram Jai Jai Ram
3. Om Sri Ram Jai Ram Jai Jai Ram
4. Om Sri Ram Jai Ram Jai Jai Ram

OM SRI RAM JAI RAM JAI JAI RAM, OM SRI RAM JAI RAM JAI JAI RAM, OM

Form circles of five with, if possible, three women and two men or three men and two women. At the end of the second repetition of the entire cycle, the 'twos' exchange places.

1. Join hands in circles of five and move to the right.
2. Continue holding hands and swing arms.
3. Alternate hands: Releasing held hands, open arms wide, reach in front of people immediately to either side and take the outstretched hands of those people just beyond on either side.
4. Duck under raised alternate hands (joined hands are brought over the heads and lowered to behind the shoulders).

To end the dance, remain in the last position (movement 4). The leader may quicken the tempo and direct the dancers to lean back slightly. With all standing in place, say "Om Hari Om."

RAM NAM MELODY

On the recording is heard Amina Erickson singing the Ram Nam as she learned it from Mother Krishnabai who lived at Anandashram (Abode of Bliss) in Kanhangad, South India. Mother Krishnabai received this mantra from Papa Ramdas who attained God-realization through the repetition of this sacred phrase. With the passing of Mother Krishnabai in 1989, Swami Satchitananda of Anandashram continues their work of encouraging the use of this mantra as a means to realization and world peace.

This Ram Nam melody became the basis for the Ram Nam Pranam Partners Dance (directions follow). This may be done successfully in either the original 3/4 waltz tempo or in 4/4.

RAM NAM PRANAM DANCE FOR PART-
NERS
(For partners, Key of C, open tuning)

1. Sri Ram
2. Jai Ram
3. Jai Jai Ram Om
4. Sri Ram
5. Jai Ram
6. Jai Jai Ram Om

(God who at once is truth and power, impersonal and personal! Victory to Thee! Victory, victory to Thee!)

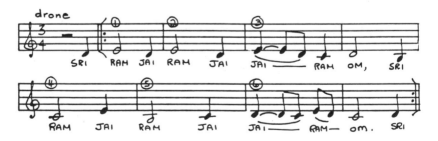

Pranam is a greeting in recognition of the divine essence within each person. One bows deeply, holding the hands palm to palm at the heart. In a traditional greeting, it is often accompanied by the phrase "Namaste"—greeting the divine in the one met. Begin by taking partners and form a circle.

1. Bow to partner.
2. All make a half-turn and bow to corner (person standing on the other side, who is not one's partner).
3. Turn in place to the right with the arms raised. Bow to the center on "Om."
4. Bow to corner.
5. Bow to partner.
6. Turn in place to the left with the arms raised. Bow to the center on "Om."

All quickly step past their partner to a new partner and the dance begins again.

As the dance continues, the leader may quicken the tempo at the beginning of each cycle. The leader may also introduce an alternate movement: instead of bowing, the hands touch the heart and open wide. Return to the original tempo for a repetition or two before ending the dance.

MELODIC RAM NAM
(Key of C, open tuning)

1. Sri Ram Jai Ram Jai Jai Ram
2. Sri Ram Jai Ram Jai Jai Ram
3. Sri Ram Jai Ram Jai Jai Ram
4. Sri Ram Jai Ram Jai Jai Ram

This Dance is for one or more (concentric) circles.

1. All join hands and move to the left.

2. Alternate hands: Release held hands, open arms wide, reach in front of the people immediately to either side and take the outstretched hands of those people just beyond on both sides.

3. Raise alternate hands toward the center of the circle, just above shoulder level, forming a many pointed star.

4. Duck under raised arms: joined hands are brought over the heads and lowered behind the shoulders.

After a few repetitions, the leader calls for men to sing and women to chant "Om." On the next cycle, the leader calls for women to sing and men to chant "Om." This alternation continues until the leader calls for all to sing together.

To conclude the dance, at the end of a cycle the leader calls for all to 'hold this position.' All sing 3. and 4. while maintaining the last position (movement 4.). Standing in place, all sing "Om Hari Om."

BENEDICTION DANCE

(Key of C, open tuning, or Cm, standard tuning)

1. May the blessings of God rest upon you.
2. May God's peace abide with you.
3. May God's presence
4. Illuminate your heart
5. Now and forever more.

This benediction was given by Pir-O-Murshid Hazrat Inayat Khan as part of the Universal Worship service. In this dance, everyone gives as well as receives the blessing.

All take partners. Partners will stand in place while exchanging this blessing. Dancers will progress in the direction they now face, past their partner, to meet a new partner.

1. Partners face each other. To begin, the arms are raised above the head with the palms facing the partner. As the first line is sung, the arms are lowered, out to each side and down, as in blessing.

2. Partners join hands at waist level and impart peace through their glance.

3. Partners release hands and raise arms above their head, palms

up, in invocation of the Divine presence.

4. Place right hand on partner's heart and left hand over partner's hand.

5. Partners bow to each other, with hands held palm to palm at their heart. Partners progress and the dance begins again.

To conclude, all face the center of the circle and sing through one complete cycle with slightly altered movements; all join hands in a circle on movement 2., the right hand is extended toward the center of the circle on movement 4. All other movements are the same.

UNIVERSAL WORSHIP DANCE AND ROUND
(Key of C, open tuning)

1. Sri Ram   (Hindu name for God)
2. Ahura Mazda   (Zoroastrian name for God as Indestructible Wisdom)
3. Buddha   (Enlightened Oneness)
4. Ya-Hu-Weh (or Yah)   (Most exalted Hebrew name for God)
5. Eleison   (Greek phrase, invoking Divine Mercy)
6. Allah   (Name of God in Islam)
7. Toward the One

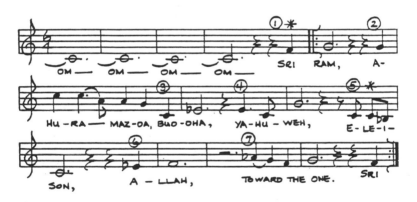

This dance combines phrases from the six religions originally celebrated in the Universal Worship.

With regard to the sacred phrase from the Hebrew tradition, Murshid Samuel Lewis (raised a Jew) felt that it was important to begin to recover the mystical power of this name in order to bring vitality back into the tradition. In most Jewish circles this is still not considered acceptable. Murshid's friend, Rabbi Zalman Schachter, has recommended that for use in the Dances of Universal Peace, the men could sing the "Yah" part of the phrase and the women "Hu-weh." In this fashion, no one person says the whole sacred name, but all may benefit by hearing it. Or, where it is not expedient to teach this, he recommends simply substituting "Yah" for the whole phrase. This is better, he feels, than changing it to Adonai, a name translated as "Lord."

Round: This round is made up of fragments of ancient melodies lifted from their old places into one long new phrase. Round entrances are marked with a star.

Dance: This dance may also be done as a round if there are two or four circles. It is is done slowly but in rhythm; dancers step slowly in rhythm and are in constant motion as the movements flow smoothly from one to the next. Begin with all facing the center of the circle.

1. Bow deeply to the center of the circle with the hands held palm to palm in front of the heart. Pranam is the traditional Hindu greeting in recognition of the divine essence within each person.

2. All turn to face counterclockwise and walk slowly (one step to each down beat) in the line of direction with hands held above the head in the symbol of the sacred fire or sun disk. The palms face forward with the tips of the index fingers and thumbs touching to form a triangle.

3. Continuing to walk forward, hold hands palm to palm. Lightly and briefly touch the middle of the forehead with the base of the thumbs. Then briefly hold the hands just in front of the throat and briefly in front of the heart, with a slight bow. This is a traditional Buddhist mudra invoking, respectively, the Buddha (Oneness), the Dharma (teachings) and the Sangha (spiritual community).

4. Continuing to walk forward, hands extend out from the heart with the palms open as if holding open the Book of Divine Law.

5. Continuing to walk forward, the arms reach up and out in a

gesture of receptivity.

6. Spin to the right with hands held high, in unity with the All.

7. Face the center of the circle, stand in place and extend the hands toward the center of the circle.

The dance begins again. To conclude, at the end of a cycle the leader calls for all to join hands and chant "Om" while sidestepping. If the dance is being done as a round, the first circle chants "Om" while the second circle completes their cycle. Then all chant "Om" eight times and sing "Toward the One" with the hands extended toward the center of the circle.

KWAN ZEON BOSAI DANCE
(Key of C, open tuning)

1. Kwan Zeon Bosai
2. Kwan Zeon Bosai
3. Kwan Zeon Bosai
4. Kwan Zeon Bo

Kwan Yin is the Chinese name for the Bodhisattva of Compassion. In the Far East, this Bodhisattva is female; Avalokitesvara is an associated male form. The ideographs which in Mandarin Chinese are pronounced Kwan-yin, are pronounced Kwan-on in Korean and Kan-on in modern Japanese. Kwan-ze-on (Korean) and Kan-ze-on (Japanese) are a variant of this name.

In this form the name means, "She who perceives (Kwan) the sounds (on) of the world (ze);" that is she who witnesses the distress of beings in the world, who hears their cries, and accords them mercy. "Bosai" is the same as Bosatsu (Japanese) or Bodhisattva (Sanskrit).

All form a circle facing the line of direction. The circle will move in a clockwise direction with the dancers walking forward during all movements.

First time through:
1. Walking in the line of direction clockwise, the hands are held

palm to palm above the head.

2. Hands are held palm to palm at the forehead (in front of the third eye center).

3. Hands are held palm to palm at the heart.

4. Hands slowly move down to waist level and out to either side, in blessing.

Second time through:

1. Continuing to walk in the line of direction clockwise, the left hand is placed on the right shoulder of the person in front. The right arm is extended and raised to above the center of the circle with the palm up. The glance is toward the fingertips of the right hand throughout this cycle.

2. The right arm is lowered slightly (to about forehead level).

3. The right arm is lowered still more so that it is extended horizontally at heart level toward the center of the circle.

4. Turn right hand palm down and slowly lower arm in blessing.

Third time through:

1, 2, 3: Continuing to walk in the line of direction clockwise, the arms are held as if cradling an infant. This infant can be seen as the first person who comes to mind, the wounded child in oneself, a person one knows to be in need, one's family or community, or as the entire world. The arms may gradually expand to include more so that the final movement flows naturally from it.

4. On the final "Bo," the arms are lowered with the palms extended down and out to either side as in blessing. The third phase of the Dance is reminiscent of the Buddhist walking meditation in which one feels that one is walking on the heads of all sentient beings, with each step a blessing.

The dance begins again and ends at the leader's discretion.

NEMBUTSU (NAMO AMIDA BUTSU)
(For partners, Key of C, open tuning)

Namo Amida Butsu   ("Homage to the Buddha of
Namo Amida Butsu   Infinite Light, Wisdom
Namo Amida Butsu   and Compassion.")
Namo Amida Butsu
This is another of Murshid Samuel Lewis' original Dances. All

take partners. The circle will move in a counterclockwise direction. The phrase is repeated four times for each movement. The leader will need to call out each change of movement as the Dance progresses, at least through the first cycle.

    1. All walk in the line of direction counterclockwise with the following hand movement: With the left hand over the right, held at waist level toward the outside of the circle, clap four times in rhythm with "Namo Amida." Clap once toward the center of the circle with the right hand over the left on "But-." Clap once toward the outside of the circle with the left hand over the right on "-su." Repeat four times.

    2. Continue to walk counterclockwise with the hand positions reversed. Clap four times toward the center of the circle, with the right hand over the left, once to the outside of the circle and once toward the center. Repeat four times.

    3. All face partners. One partner will walk backward in the circle and the other forward. Clap both hands lightly against partner's hands in the same rhythm as above. Repeat four times.

    4. All make a half-turn to face their corner. (If partner is on one's

left hand in the circle, corner is person on one's right hand.) Those who were walking forward will now walk backward and those who were walking backward will now walk forward. Clap hands with corner as above. Repeat four times.

5. All face the line of direction counterclockwise. Walk with arms crossed over the heart for four repetitions.

6. With the arms crossed and palms facing out, all face their partner and clap hands as in movement 3. Repeat four times.

7. With arms crossed and palms facing out, all turn to face their corner and clap hands. Repeat four times.

8. Join right hands with corner (elbow is slightly bent so hands are above elbow level) and circle each other, repeating the phrase four times. The leader may increase the tempo slightly for this and the next three movements.

9. Join left hands with corner and circle each other, repeating the phrase four times.

10. Return to partner, join right hands and circle each other for four repetitions.

11. Join left hands with partner; circle each other for four repetitions.

Dance returns to original tempo at this point if it was speeded up for the last four movements.

To begin another cycle, the leader asks for the left hand person of each partnership to progress counterclockwise two places to stand between two new people and begin again with movement 1. The musicians continue to play during this progression at the original tempo.

To conclude the Dance:

12. All walk in the line of direction counterclockwise for eight repetitions. The following hand movement (Dharani) is done once for each repetition. Begin with the hands palm to palm above the head and slowly lower the hands. At waist level, move the hands out to each side with the palms facing down. Turn the palms up and slowly raise the arms until the hands are again palm to palm above the head. On the last repetition, the hands remain at waist level

with the palms down to each side.

To conclude, all may bow toward the center while saying "Sowaka" (meaning "Svaha" or "so be it").

Variation: This dance may also be done without partners using movements 1, 2, 5, and 12 in sequence.

BISMILLAH YA FATTAH DANCE AND ROUND

(For partners, Key of C, open tuning)

1. Bismillah   In the name (or with the light) of Allah
2. Bismillah
3. Ya Fattah   Opener of the Way
4. Ya Fattah
5. Allah
6. Ya Fattah

In this dance, partners greet each other in the name of Unity, with the wish that the way or path be made clear for each other.

If there are enough people present to form two or four concentric circles, this dance may also be done as a round. Round entrances are marked with a star. All face a partner in their circle. Dancers will progress to new partners in the direction they now face.

1. Join right hands with first partner and walk past this partner.

2. Join left hands with second partner and walk past this partner.

3. Face third partner. Hands touch one's heart and open wide in a rapid movement on the "-tah", like a door opening.

4. Make a half-turn back to face second partner; open arms wide as above.

5. Spin to the right, with arms raised.

6. All face the center of the circle. Hands touch the heart and open wide in a rapid movement on the "-tah."

Dance begins again with the third partner of the last cycle becoming the first partner of the next cycle.

GOD OF BEAUTY ROUND
(Key of C)

"Peace will come to the Middle East when Muslims, Christians and Jews eat together, dance together and pray together to the glory of the One God," said Murshid Samuel Lewis. This song melds the sacred names of God from these three religious traditions with an invocation of beauty in a simple, yet beautiful, two-part round.

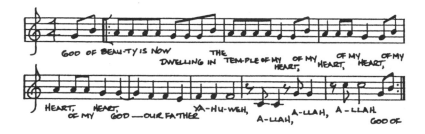

WHAT WONDROUS LOVE
(Key of G, standard tuning)

Many people are familiar with this traditional Shaker hymn. In

this contrapuntal version, it is best to sing with a guitar or piano and divide into male and female voices. The fifth repetition of the phrase, "Ishk Allah Mahbud Lillah," needs careful rehearsal. This phrase translates: "God is the love, the lover and the beloved," or "The love, lover, and beloved are One." An improvised interlude of any nature can be played between verses.

SUBHAN ALLAH
(C drone)

"Subhan Allah" translates to "Allah is Pure." This arranged

composition recalls the purity of voice and heart found in Gregor-ian chants.

A drone instrument, (a tamboura is especially nice) should continue throughout the entire piece, even through the modulation in the chorale. Begin by singing the wazifa on the tonic (home) note for a few minutes. This helps to bring the music into focus.

YA AZ'M ROUND DANCE
(For partners, Key of D, standard tuning)

1. Ya Az'm
2. Hu, Hu
3. Allah Hu, Allah Hu
4. Allah Hu, Allah Hu
5. Hu, Hu, Hu,
   Hu, Hu, Hu,
   Hu, Hu, Hu, Hu.
6. As-salaam aleikum
   Wa-aleikum as-salaam

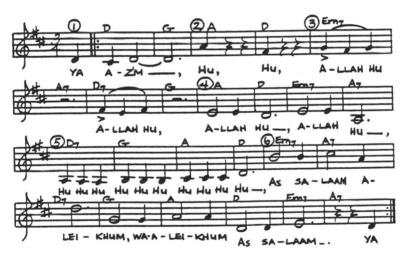

"Ya Az'm" is a greeting of the dervishes. This is a Persian pronunciation of the wazifa "Ya Azim," meaning "O Thou, Highest of the High." As used in this dance, the greeting means: "How wonderfully does Allah manifest through you." One literal translation of "Allah Hu" is "Allah, Him/Herself." "Hu" is the most sacred sound of the Islamic tradition and survives as a sacred phrase from the Native Middle Eastern tradition preceding and underlying Judaism, Christianity and Islam.

Round: The phrase construction of this four-part round is irregular but the entrances (marked with a star) come regularly at six-bar intervals.

Dance: All face a partner in their circle. Dancers will progress to a new partner in the direction they now face. If the dance is also performed as a round, form two circles of partners and bring the second group in at the third star in the music.

1. Partners face each other with their right hand covering their own heart on "Ya." On "Az'm," they bow in greeting to each other as the right hand moves down and out to the right side.

2. Partners circle each other clockwise. On the first "Hu," the arms are raised with palms facing but not touching partner's palms. On the second "Hu," the arms are lowered with the palms facing the earth.

3. Spin individually to the right and then to the left.

4. Partners circle clockwise. Arms are raised with palms facing but not touching partner's palms on "Allah" and lowered on "Hu."

5. Spin individually to the right with the hands moving as if patting the earth.

6. Join hands with partner, raise arms and circle in waltz tempo clockwise. The arms are lowered with a slight bow on the first "kum" and then raised again.

Progress to next partner and the dance begins again. Dance ends with all facing the center of the circle and singing "Ya Az'm."

DERVISH CYCLE, PART I
(Key of C, open tuning)

This selection on the recording is the first of a cycle of three dances in what is called the "Dervish Cycle." These were among the first dances presented by Murshid Samuel Lewis. In this recording, Murshid is heard leading this dance which is based on an Egyptian dervish zikr that he participated in while in Cairo in 1960-61.

The instructions and musical notation for the complete Dervish Cycle are given on page 126.

ALLAH UNISON CHANT

A short piece by the Sufi Choir, chanting this name of God.

YA HAYY YA HAQQ
(Key of G, open tuning)

Group Singing Practice: This translates as "O Life, O Truth." On the recording is a composed version which must be carefully rehearsed, especially by the conductor. The following directions are for a good, improvised version. Divide the singers into two groups, left and right, and establish the three-beat rhythm with a drum. The leader then conducts one group in "Ya Hayy" and the other in "Ya Haqq," improvising entrances, switching the phrases from one group to the other, lengthening and shortening the phrases and end with all in unison.

HYMN TO THE PROPHET
(Key of C, open tuning)

This devotional song is Arabic in origin. The phrase: "As-salaatu, wa-salaamu aleikha, Ya Rassoul Allah, Ya Habib Allah," translates to:

"Our prayers and wishes for peace be with you and from you, O Messenger, O Beloved of God."

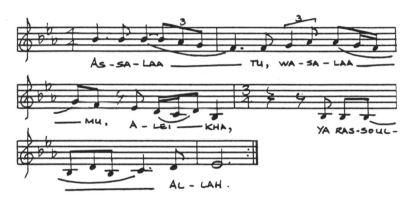

DERVISH CYCLE OF DANCES
(Key of C, open tuning)

This three-part dance is usually done as a complete cycle. A deeper level of concentration is required for this dance than for some of the others and is best done in a group that has established some level of attunement.

I: ALLAH YA HAYY YA HAQQ

1. Allah, Allah
2. Ya Hayy, Ya Haqq (O Life, O Truth)

1. All join hands in one circle and sidestep as follows: right foot to the right side on "Al-", left foot to meet the right on "-lah." Repeat this. The third repetition of "Allah" is to the left: left foot to the left side on "Al-", right foot to meet the right on "-lah." Repeat this. Alternate from the right to the left side throughout the dance. (Alternate movement: one step to the right and one step to the left.)

2. While the circle continues this movement, the leader selects a partner to join him/her in the center of the circle. They face each other and slowly circle clockwise. Without touching, the arms are raised high on "Ya Hayy" and lowered on "Ya Haqq." This is repeated at least four times, after which the leader leaves the center. The first partner selects a new partner and begins this movement again.

This is continued until everyone has been in the center or until the leader ends this portion of the dance by saying "Amin." (Amen, which means "so be it.")

Note: With beginners, the leader may choose to remain in the center, selecting partners one by one. Or the leader may stand near the musicians (off to one side within the circle) and maintain the proper rhythm and tempo. If the group is very large, the leader may have more than one partnership circling at one time, beginning each set him/herself or designating an advanced student to do so.

II: EL ALLAH HU

1. El Allah Hu   (Allah alone exists)
2. Allah Hu

1. All join hands in one circle. While standing in place, each person moves his/her head in a triangular pattern: head turns to the right shoulder on "El," to the left shoulder on "Allah," then lowered, directing the "Hu" into the heart. (Alternate movement: raise the head, face upwards, on "Allah.")

2. While the circle continues this movement, the leader selects a partner to join her/him in the center of the circle. They join right hands and circle each other while chanting "Allah Hu," with the head raised up on "Allah" and lowered on "Hu." After several repetitions, they end by bowing to each other. The leader rejoins the outer circle while the partner selects a new partner.

Variations: The two dancers in the center may vary this movement, with the first person taking the lead. After having joined right hands for a while, they may switch to left hands or join both hands, with one arm crossed over the other. The pace of repetition in the center may become quite fast without losing control. The outer circle continues at the same tempo and forms the stability which allows for this freedom.

Note: The leader may choose to bring in all partners her/ himself. This requires considerable skill and attunement.

In a group composed of a teacher and his/her students, the teacher may offer the practice of transmitting through movement and voice a very definite feeling to the partner selected which this person then passes on to his/her next partner. This is not usually done in public dance classes and is part of advanced dance training.

The dance ends at the discretion of the leader, usually after all have been in the center if the group is small.

III: Hu Whirl

1. Allah Hu
2. Hu

1. All join hands in one circle. There are three variations of movement in the outer circle for the phrase "Allah Hu":

One: In place, all raise joined hands on "Allah" and lower them on "Hu."

Two: All face the line of direction counterclockwise and place the right hand on the left shoulder of the person in front. Step forward on the right foot with the head turned toward the center of the circle and slightly raised on "Allah." Step forward on the left foot with the head turned toward the center of the circle and lowered on "Hu."

Three: All face the center of the circle with hands on the shoulders of those on either side. The head is raised and lowered as in the previous movement. If the circle is large enough, place arms around each other, shoulders close together.

The leader alternates these movements of the outer circle by calling out 'One,' 'Two,' or 'Three.'

2. While the circle continues its movement, the leader goes to the center of the circle. After a slight bow, the leader spins with the arms opened wide while intoning a long and sustained "Hu." The leader then chooses another person to spin.

It is possible to spin for long periods of time without losing control or getting dizzy. The eyes are kept open while spinning and the leader may have to remind the dancers to do so. Centering or focusing the awareness in the heart center will also help. Each dancer may spin as fast or slow or as long as is comfortable. For beginners, this may be as long as one exhalation.

The leader should be ready to help those who become dizzy by offering them a steadying hand or helping them back into the outer circle. At the completion of the spin, the dancer may stand for a moment with the arms crossed over the chest, fingertips resting on the shoulders, with the gaze fixed at the cross of the arms until any dizziness passes.

Beginners may be directed to feel the heart radiating outward as they spin. Advanced students may be taught to spin in attunement with the various centers, elements, planets or prophets.

This dance continues until all have been in the center or as long as the leader feels is appropriate. To conclude, the leader calls for movement 'two' after asking the last person in the center to rejoin the outer circle. All chant "Hu" (usually in multiples of 16), stepping once for each "Hu," gradually speeding up until the leader calls, "All spin!". All spin individually while intoning an extended "Hu" from the heart.

YA JAMIL

(Key of Em, acappella)

One of the ninety-nine names of Allah, this phrase means "God is beautiful and loves beauty." This four-part round is sung acappella with a concentration on beauty. Round entrances are marked with a star.

JESUS IS OUR SUN

(Key of C)

1. Jesus is our sun, our sun is Jesus shining.
2. Er Rahman, Er Rahim (Compassion and Mercy)

On the first line, divide the women into sopranos and altos and have the men sing in unison. For the second line, divide the men into tenor and bass. For a mantric effect, sing the first line twice and the second line three times. Continue with this alternation.

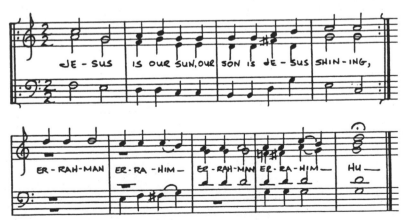

SOUND PRACTICE

The Sufi Choir here performs a sound practice demonstrating the perfect cadence of Western music. The overtones of a tonic note are transposed to fit the human voice and what is formed is the fundamental expression of Western harmony.

YA-HU-WEH

Recorded here is another sound practice using the most sacred name of God in the Hebrew tradition. Murshid Samuel Lewis felt that modern Jews would come to the realization of their true being when they remembered the forgotten devotion of chanting God's name as essence rather than as attribute.

As noted under the Universal Worship Dance, there is some controversy on this point in the Jewish community. Rabbi Zalman Schachter, Murshid's friend and a leader of the Jewish Renewal movement has recommended that in some groups it may be better to have the men sing "Ya-" and the women "Hu-Weh", so that both can hear the sacred sound but no one individual says it. He has said that when the male-female split in Judaism is healed, then also the Name will be restored as whole.

SHALOM ALEICHEM
(For partners, Key of C, open tuning)

1. Shalom Aleichem, Shalom Aleichem (Peace be with you)
2. Shalom, Shalom
3. Shalom Aleichem, Shalom Aleichem
4. Shalom, Shalom

Shalom in Hebrew is equivalent to the Arabic word Salaam, meaning peace.   In fact, they are both from an older Aramaic root of the same meaning which has been used throughout recorded history in the Middle East. In this dance, partners greet each other in peace.

All take partners. Dancers will progress past this partner in the direction they now face to meet a new partner.

1. Join hands with partner and circle clockwise. The arms are raised during "Shalom Alei-" and lowered on "chem."
2. Spin individually to the right with the arms raised.
3. Rejoin hands with partner and circle counterclockwise.
4. Spin individually to the left and progress to next partner.
Dance begins again. Unless the circle is very large, continue

until at least a full round of progressions through the circle is completed. The dance may continue longer if the circle is small.

The tempo may be gradually increased until the feeling is quite joyful, then decreased, which adds a note of longing. Usually, the tempo of the last one or two repetitions are done slowly, allowing the dancers to absorb the energy, peace, joy and longing that this traditional melody transmits.

If numbers permit forming two or four circles, this dance may be done as a two or four part round. In a two part round, the second circle enters halfway through (at 3.) In a four part round, each circle enters respectively at 1., 2., 3., and 4. Conclude with one cycle in unison.

KALAMA DANCE

(Key of C, open tuning)

1. La illaha   (There is no God
2. El Allah Hu   but God)
   Repeat a total of three times
3. Mohammed-ar-rassoul-lillah   (Mohammed is the
4. Mohammed-ar-rassoul-lillah   messenger of God)

The recording begins with Murshid Samuel Lewis leading this dance, one of his originals. It then cuts to a later version recorded in 1974 with the added counter-point.

This phrase of the zikr, "La illaha el Allah Hu," is from an Egyptian dialect of Arabic. Another translation of this phrase is "There is none but the One." The second part of the phrase is traditional in Islam and invokes Mohammed as a messenger or channel of God. In the Sufi esotericism, this phrase offers an opportunity to imbibe the spirit of Mohammed as one who embodied a "complete human being" (<u>Insaan-i-Kamil</u>), that is, one who could include all realms of consciousness—from the most subtle to the most material—in his everyday awareness.

In this regard, dancers may be encouraged to feel the fulfillment of their own Divine purpose or <u>risalat</u>, which is the essence of <u>rassoul</u> in each person. During the spins, dancers may also be directed to feel they are God's instrument for bringing the message of unity and peace into the world. As in all of these dances, the true meaning is to be found in one's experience. When one sets an intention it should be as open-ended as possible to allow dancers' experiences to exceed that of the leader.

All join hands in a circle.

1. Step backward, away from the center of the circle, with a slight bow in an attitude of emptying and letting go of limitation and separation.

2. Step toward the center of the circle, raising held hands in affirmation of the One Being, the Divine Unity.

Movements 1. and 2. are repeated a total of three times.

3. Spin individually in place, clockwise, with the arms raised. The spins may be deliberately slowed in order to feel the nobility and grandeur as characterized by the Sufi ideal of Mohammed as Insaan-i-Kamil, a perfect or all-inclusive human being.

4. Spin individually counterclockwise.

Dance begins again.

This dance may also be performed with the counterpoint which requires a strong familiarity with the music. Directions follow:

COUNTERPOINT TO THE KALAMA DANCE

(For partners, Key of C, open tuning)

1. Allah
2. Allah
3. Mohammed-ar-rassoul-lillah
4. Allah
5. Allah
6. Mohammed-ar-rassoul-lillah
7. Allah
8. Rassoul-lillah
9. La illaha el il Allah Hu
   La illaha el Allah
   La illaha el il Allah Hu
   La illaha el Allah

Those who will perform the counterpoint take partners (usually man/woman partnerships) and form an inner circle. The woman is on the left-hand side of the partnership. The outer circle or circles will perform the regular movements to the Kalama Dance.

Dance begins with the inner circle and outer circle/s performing the Kalama Dance together twice. At the beginning of the third repetition, the inner circle begins with the counterpoint as follows:

1. With hands in prayer mudra (palm to palm) at the heart, bow to partner.

2. All make a half-turn and bow to corner. (If person on the right is one's partner, then person on the left is one's corner and vice versa.)

3. Individually spin to the right.

4. Bow to corner.

5. Bow to partner.

6. Individually spin to the left.

7. Bow to the center of the circle.

8. Women quickly progress to the left by passing inside the circle to stand on the left of a new partner. Men stand in place. All join hands and raise them while taking a step toward the center of the circle on "-lillah."

9. With hands joined, step backward on "La illaha" and forward toward the center of the circle on "el il Allah (Hu)." This is repeated for a total of four times. Then the cycle begins again.

To conclude, the leader calls for the inner circle to perform the Kalama Dance in unison with the outer circle. After two or three repetitions, the leader ends the dance.

Note: Those who are familiar with this dance or those listening to the cassette recording titled Dances of Universal Peace Volume I will notice that line 6. of the counterpoint has been changed from the original version. It is grammatically incorrect in Arabic to recite the phrase as recorded. Please use the correct phrase, "Moham-med-ar-rassoul-lillah."

FREE ALLAH

In this practice, participants are encouraged to sing the name Allah freely and openly from the heart, listening to all voices as one voice. This version was recorded at the end of a week long seminar held in the summer of 1974. Singing in the midst of open-hearted voices such as these is an ecstatic musical experience. It goes beyond music. It is just at this point that the mystic awakes. "I am sound," says the mystic, and can speak of it no longer.

A Sufi Story

In this regard, one is reminded of a Sufi story from the 13th century involving Mevlana Jelaluddin Rumi and his heart companion, Shem-ed-din Tabrizi. The following version is quoted from *The Whirling Ecstasy*, a collection of stories about Shams and Rumi written by Aflaki.

"At this time Master Jelal-ed-din was teaching science as professor of four colleges. Students walked at his stirrup. One day he had left the cotton merchants' college with a brilliant throng, and was passing the inn of the sugar merchants. Shems-ed-din rose, came forward, and grasping the bridle of his horse, shouted:

"O teacher of Muslims, was Abu Yezid or Mohammed the greater?'

The shock of this question, our Master said, was as if the seven separate heavens fell upon the earth. A great fire mounted through his body to the top of his skull, whence he saw a window open and a thin smoke rise to the foot of the celestial throne.

Master Jelal-ed-din replied:

"Mohammed, God's envoy, is the greatest of mortals. What of Abu Yezid?"

"Then," said Shems-ed-din, "what does it mean that Mohammed said: 'We have not known Thee as Thou shouldst be known,' while Abu Yezid said; 'I am exalted, my dignity is upraised, I am the sultan of sultans?'"

Our Master replied: "Abu Yezid's thirst had been quenched at one gulp; the jar of his understanding was filled with this little quantity; light was limited to the size of his window. But God's Elect sought each day further, and from hour to hour and day to day saw light and power and divine wisdom increase. This is why he said; 'We have not known Thee as Thou shouldst be known.'"

Shems-ed-din gave a cry and fell. Our Master got down from his mule, sent the imams away and gave orders to raise the sheikh. Until he came to himself, our Master held the head of Shems-ed-din upon his knees. Then he took him by the hand, and returned to the college on foot. Thereafter none had access to them.

***

How to Use this Book

We have published this book in order to help spread the Dances of Universal Peace and to provide some standardized forms of some of the essential Dances in the repertoire. We encourage you to try out these Dances within your own communities. Here are a few things we suggest as you find your way into leading the Dances.

First, before you try to lead a Dance, make sure you have experienced it. It is impossible to offer someone an experience you have not had, and the Dances are, first and foremost, a matter of experience. In addition, there is much about a given Dance that we cannot put into words, no matter how refined our description.

Second, try the published form of the Dance first before you experiment. Each Dance holds an energy, atmosphere or vibration, like a cup holds liquid. The sacred phrase (primarily), movements and music all contribute to this container. If the container is varied too much it will tend to "leak." We suggest you lead this established form several times before trying a variation. However, along with this, we acknowledge we do expect that a certain amount of experimentation will occur, especially as Dances are adapted for use with children, the developmentally challenged and other special populations. The Dances are an active, dynamic, growing and changing body of sacred communal art. Leaders who grow deep roots in the tradition contribute to even more vibrant flowering and fruit.

Third, if you find that the Dances engage your whole heart and being, and if you want to pursue the path they offer and deepen in them, this possibility is available through a system of apprenticeship and certification with a more experienced teacher. Any transmission of the sacred has always been achieved, throughout human history, in a person-to-person relationship, a living experience regardless of institutions and organizations. This aspect of the Dance and walking meditation work has been assumed by the Mentor Teachers Guild of the Dances, a group empowered by Murshid Moineddin Jablonski, the spiritual successor of Murshid Samuel L. Lewis.

Current Dance leaders are invited to join in a "traveling-with" relationship with a member of the Guild, an Apprentice Mentor or another certified teacher. The "traveling-with" (or supervision) is independent of an interest in certification or further training. However, it does involve mutual agreement to written ethical guidelines. In recommending teachers to the public, the International Center for the Dances of Universal Peace and its regional networkers give preference to certified and supervised teachers. This is because of both their expertise as well as their agreement to be ethically guided in their leadership of these powerful, transformative practices. Similarly, use of the official Dance logo of entwined hearts is limited to supervised teachers. For a full packet about the certification process, please address the International Dance Center office.

If you visit Dances of Universal Peace meetings worldwide, you should realize that Dance teachers differ dramatically in their experience, repertoire, ability, attunement and commitment. More than 400 different Dances currently exist and the body of Dances continues to grow to embrace all the sacred traditions of humanity. Some leaders know only a few Dances casually learned from a booklet or tape. Others have studied for years, have deeply pursued their own emotional and spiritual process with the Dances and have taken them as their life's work. It is natural for all levels of commitment to exist in a sacred practice which offers both surface and depth approaches, both the traditional and the radically creative.

As you seek out experiences of the Dances and further guidance in them, we urge you to connect with certified or supervised teachers whenever possible. Please write to the International Dance Center office for a referral.

May the Dances of Universal Peace inspire you to energize your own Dance of Life!

—Neil Douglas-Klotz,
for the Mentor Teachers Guild
of the Dances of Universal Peace

The Dances of Universal Peace are taught and celebrated in most of the states of the U.S., as well as in Canada, Australia, New Zealand, Japan, Brazil, Great Britain, Holland, Belgium, Germany, Austria, Switzerland, Poland, Czech Republic, Russia, Ukraine, South Africa and an increasing number of places on the planet. For a referral in your area, for information about Dance training and workshops or for a complete catalog of recordings and teaching materials, including the writings of Murshid Samuel L. Lewis
please contact the address below. All of this information, including the most up-to-date information about Dance meetings and contacts may also be found at our Internet website.

PeaceWorks
International Network for the Dances of Universal Peace
444 NE Ravenna Blvd., Suite 306
Seattle, WA 98115-6467 USA
Email: peaceworks@compuserve.com
World Wide Web:
http://www.dancesofuniversalpeace.org